About the Author

James C. Makens is a consultant in the area of Marketing and Strategic Planning. He has worked with many domestic and international corporations including R. J. Reynolds, Consolidated Foods, Quaker Oats, Pan American World Airways, Standard Fruit Co., First Union National Bank, International Harvester, Xerox, Lowe's Companies, and many more. He has also provided marketing and strategic planning seminars for many corporations and foreign government ministries including Sheraton Hotels, Travelodge of Australia, Regent Hotels of Kuala Lumpur, The Tourism Ministries of Indonesia, Singapore, and several Latin American nations.

Jim has also served as Vice President of Marketing for General Medical Centers of Anaheim, California where he had direct responsibility for all marketing and sales activities.

He is the author of three professional books in the area of marketing and management and has written many professional articles for publication including the *Journal of Marketing, Journal of Marketing Research,* and *Journal of Applied Psychology.*

He is a frequent speaker before business and professional groups and has lectured in several countries.

Dr. Makens earned a Ph.D. from Michigan State University as well as the M.B.A. and M.S. degrees. He has taught on the faculty of several universities and currently lectures at the Babcock Graduate School of Management of Wake Forest University.

Contents

Preface

A WINNING MARKETING PLAN

What this organization needs is a good marketing plan! Today these words are heard in virtually all organizations. Small companies, museums, banks, multi-billion-dollar conglomerates, universities, the Chamber of Commerce, and even government departments are calling for a marketing plan. Just yesterday it was commonly felt that a marketing plan was fine for companies such as General Motors or IBM, but was too sophisticated for everyone else. The sudden recognition of the need for a marketing plan has left seasoned and rookie managers grasping for direction.

Even MBA graduates with training in marketing usually have difficulty in knowing how to proceed. Most marketing courses and text books simply don't describe the process.

It is not surprising that organizations are now faced with a flood of documents that pose as marketing plans. In many cases, these so-called plans do not help management produce improved results and disillusionment begins.

A marketing plan must be a "winner." If the plan does not help management to gain market share, increase sales, lower marketing costs or otherwise "win," the plan was probably a waste of time.

A winning marketing plan is the result of a commitment to excellence. Anyone can write a mediocre plan. Unfortunately, management sometimes accepts a mediocre plan to the later regret of everyone.

All winning marketing plans have several common elements. They are listed and described here.

Realism: Dreams have no place in a marketing plan. Marketing managers are by nature optimistic, but unbridled optimism can lead to unrealistic expectations. If sales have been stagnant for several years, it is doubtful that a 300-percent increase will be obtained next year.

An unrealistic plan filled with high sales forecasts for all product categories may receive initial applause from management, but what happens if these forecasts fail to materialize?

In private, marketing and sales managers sometimes admit that they develop marketing plans just to please management and to meet the deadline. They go on to say that no one ever reviews the plan or holds them accountable for its contents, so they file the plan with bravado and make everyone feel good at least once per year. This is scarcely the formula for a winning plan. Realism is the key to success. This sometimes means that sales forecasts may be lower and marketing costs higher than desired.

The acceptance and use of a marketing plan by top management is a goal worthy of serious attention by every marketing manager. The task of the marketing department will be substantially more pleasant when top management accepts and judges performance against the marketing plan. This occurs only when the plan is realistic.

Completeness: At first appearance, the amount of information called for in a marketing plan seems to be overpowering. If your marketing plans have traditionally been written on the backs of envelopes or napkins at lunch, then the task will be substantial.

As a company builds internal systems to collect and analyze marketing-related data, the task becomes easier. The task of obtaining data may become easier but the requirement for complete data is never eliminated.

Winning marketing plans depend upon thoroughness. If loopholes remain, competitors will fill them. A marketing plan should reflect the best thinking of marketing professionals in your organization. Their thoroughness in analyzing market conditions and selecting proper strategies and detailed tactics will be reflected in market results.

Detail: Attention to detail is often the only difference between success and failure in the marketplace. Advertising schedules must be adhered to. New members of the sales force must be hired and trained on time. Budgets must reflect costs that the marketing department will face. If details are left to someone else, or if they are ignored, a company's success will be strictly the result of luck. Professional marketing is not a spinning roulette wheel.

Easy-to-follow: A marketing plan filled with endless pages of prose may be creative, but may also be a waste of time. Marketing managers sometimes forget the purpose of a written marketing plan. This is not an opportunity to quote Shakespeare or engage in a lengthy analysis of the world's political and economic problems. A marketing plan for a machine shop in North Carolina contained several pages of commentary about Margaret Thatcher. Neither Mrs. Thatcher nor anyone else in Great Britain were potential customers of this firm, nor were they likely to affect the company's strategies.

A marketing plan must be easy to read and easy to follow. If it is filled with narrative, the major points will not be read. Marketing managers with scientific or technical training sometimes use complicated flow diagrams, logarithmic charts, and mathematical equations in their marketing plans. These are often not understood by others and may contribute to confusion rather than to clarity. Remember, a marketing plan is a tool for improving communication, and a tool for guiding managerial action. It is not designed to be a great masterpiece of science and literature.

Annual–Regular: The process of developing and using a marketing plan cannot be accomplished on the basis of, "When we get around to doing it." Winning marketing plans are annual and are developed during the same time period each year.

It is essential to set aside a block of time. This should precede the date for implementation of the plan by at least one month. Many companies complete this task several months in advance of their fiscal or calendar years. Development of the marketing plan and the financial budget must be synchronized.

The annual marketing plan is always best developed away from the office. A conference center, lodge, or other environment with a minimum of distractions serves as an excellent setting to achieve productivity when writing a marketing plan.

Desire by Top Management: The commitment of top management to a marketing plan is essential. Unfortunately, in some organizations top management does not believe in the planning process, and feels that a marketing plan is a waste of time. A marketing manager who believes in the use of a marketing plan will face extreme frustration and stress in this type of organization. In many cases, top management has never fully understood the meaning of marketing and continues to equate this term with sales. A marketing plan may be thought of as a sales plan and nothing more.

Motivation within the marketing department is enhanced when top management understands the importance of marketing, desires a plan, and uses it to judge the level of success or failure of the marketing department.

Commitment of Marketing Personnel: Subordinates in the marketing department are sometimes the most difficult within the company to convince that a marketing plan is helpful. It is not unusual to discover that marketing personnel have sabotaged the marketing planning process. This is particularly troublesome when the individuals are valued and talented members of the department. Marketing personnel often are slow to accept a marketing plan, and do so only after they are convinced the process will assist them. It is important to involve marketing personnel in the development of the plan.

The involvement of subordinates is always influenced by the commitment of top management. If the plan is not used by management, marketing personnel will be the first to recognize this lack of follow-through and brand the process as corporate game playing. Subsequent commitment to future marketing plans by subordinates will be limited, and the entire process may eventually be scrapped.

Custom Design: All marketing plans must be custom-made and must reflect annual changes. Beware of a marketing plan that never changes, or one that is a copy of a competitor's.

Marketing managers are often hired from competitors. It is generally a mistake for these managers to follow the objectives, strategies, and tactics of their former employer.

The market is dynamic. There are a variety of economic, political, and competitive environments that require different objectives and strategies. The financial conditions of companies worsen or improve. Managements change and so do consumers. A stagnant, copy-cat marketing plan is not realistic; it is usually a shortcut to disaster.

Written by User: A winning marketing plan is best written by those who have responsibility for its implementation. Consultants, corporate staff, and top management may be very helpful in *developing* a plan, but they should never have total responsibility for *writing* it.

Remember, a marketing plan is worthless if it is not used. Those who will be judged by the degree of success or failure in implementing a marketing plan must have responsibility for its development.

Marketing managers who allow or encourage other departments or individuals outside their control to write a marketing plan are inviting problems. This is a formula for conflict, unnecessary stress, and poor marketing productivity.

Top management has the responsibility for final approval of a marketing plan and usually requires changes. These are seldom greeted with applause from the marketing department, but must be followed. This may not be viewed as a perfect situation by the marketing department but it is superior to accepting carte blanche a marketing plan developed entirely by others.

Use by Management and Other Departments: A winning marketing plan is not for the exclusive use by the marketing department. Marketing interfaces with many departments within a company. The finance department has an integral relationship as the plan describes forecasted sales and marketing costs critical to cash flow management.

Production objectives and quotas are hollow figures unless they are synchronized with marketing. The hiring of marketing personnel must be coordinated with the personnel department. Many other departments are directly affected by the contents of a marketing plan.

Ultimate responsibility for all areas of the company is in the hands of top management. Their task can be greatly aided through the use of a marketing plan. Top management has the responsibility to thoroughly review the annual marketing plan and *to hold the marketing department responsible for objectives, sales forecasts, costs, and other critical areas of the plan.*

The marketing department must have the freedom and flexibility to modify strategies and change tactics. However, once the plan is approved by top management, the marketing department does not have the authority to change objectives or dramatically alter budgets. Any changes in these critical areas can be made only after consultation with and approval by top management. The marketing plan may be viewed as a contract between management and the marketing department.

Improved–Modified: A winning marketing plan must be continuously modified and improved. An end-of-year review will always reveal ways in which the plan can be improved.

A review of marketing plans used by a company over a five-year period should reveal change. If marketing plans look remarkably similar from year to year, the creativity and aggressiveness of the marketing department should be questioned. New marketing opportunities and challenges exist even in markets that are commonly regarded as stable and unexciting. Federal Express discovered a new way to deliver mail, the Japanese discovered that the big three American automakers were not invincible, and poultry producers discovered that a commodity item could be marketed as a differentiated branded product.

"Marketing Driven" is a phrase used with increasingly regularity to describe the leading companies and organizations in all fields. A serious and winning marketing plan is the only road map available to managers within a marketing-driven environment.

SUMMARY: A Winning Marketing Plan

Winner	Loser
Realistic	Unrealistic
Complete	Incomplete
Detailed	Loose–not detailed
Easy-to-follow	Complex
Annual–regular	Irregular
Desired by Top Management	Unimportant to Top Management
Has commitment of marketing personnel	Has mixed or no commitment
Custom-made	Copied from others
Written by user	Written by others–Consultant; Top Management
Used by Management	Not followed by Management
Improved–modified yearly	Unchanged from year to year

What This Book Can Do for You

PURPOSE OF AN OPERATIONAL MARKETING PLAN

Operational Plan. This workbook was designed to assist in the development of an operational marketing plan. The purpose of an operational marketing plan is to serve as a detailed road map for the planning and supervision of all marketing activities for the following year.

An operational marketing plan is:

1. Valid for only one year. It must be rewritten each year. In a few stable industries marketing plans may not vary much from one year to the next, but the plan is still a one-year plan.

2. Practical, results oriented. It does not deal with theory; it deals with facts. A concept such as the decay curve for consumer recall of advertisements can seldom be used in an operational marketing plan. It is also difficult to employ the product life cycle concept in an operational marketing plan. These concepts and others may be valuable to management in understanding the behavior of markets and in long-range planning, but they seldom can be directly used in an operational plan.

3. A road map for management. An operational plan is the best road map available to management to assist in charting the proper course for marketing activities during the next year. This plan might not work for any other company in the world. No two companies are exactly alike. A plan that works for you might lead to disaster for your competitors.

4. Confidential and the property of the company. An operational marketing plan tells anyone who reads it what you expect to accomplish next year and the strategy and tactics you intend to use. A competitor could easily create havoc in your marketplace with this information.

A marketing plan is the sole property of the company and does not belong to any employee regardless of tenure or title. Limited copies should be made and these should be held in a secure place by selected members of management. Occasionally, a marketing plan is copied and removed from the company. This action should be dealt with by the company attorneys.

A marketing plan is a serious document. Treating the plan as such will engender a professional and positive attitude among all company employees.

TIPS FOR WRITING A MARKETING PLAN

This manual provides a step-by-step approach to writing a marketing plan. A complete marketing plan involves many details and even the most experienced marketing manager can easily forget or overlook critical areas. This manual was designed to help marketing managers develop a marketing plan in a systematic and orderly fashion.

Marketing plans are usually given to top management for final approval. By using the approach shown in this manual, chances for receiving approval by top management should be greatly enhanced.

Remember that all companies operate differently and it may be necessary to modify various sections of this guide to meet your needs. An effective marketing plan must be custom-made for each company.

Here are tips to remember when writing a marketing plan to ensure success.

1. Keep accurate records. Good marketing plans begin by analyzing what is currently happening and what has happened in the past. It is impossible to develop solid plans for the future if the current situation is not clearly understood.

2. Allow sufficient time to write the plan. A good marketing plan cannot be written overnight. In most cases, several weeks of detailed analysis and strategy planning are required. If your records are current and orderly, the time necessary to write the plan will be reduced.

3. Assign someone to assist with the details. Marketing managers usually do not enjoy this kind of work. The task of assembling sales records, compiling statistics, computing percentages, and gathering market intelligence can be done by others. A well-trained secretary can often perform many of these tasks. A management trainee can receive valuable experience through this process and can often make worthwhile suggestions for improving the procedure.

4. Convince other departments to analyze and provide information in a form that is useful to the marketing department. The accounting and management information systems departments can often provide information in a form which is more useful to marketing. The key is to gain their cooperation.

5. Set aside time to critically analyze the factual–statistical portion of the plan. Ask yourself, what do these figures mean? What is occurring?

It may be necessary to establish a special session for finalizing the marketing plan in a setting away from the office. This can be done in a hotel, lodge, or other facility.

6. Devote maximum attention to the development of appropriate strategies to meet next year's marketing objectives. The task of gathering and analyzing the essential data can be so time-consuming that the most critical portion of the marketing plan becomes a last-minute crash attempt to get something down on paper.

   Well-thought-out strategies are the key to success. They cannot be dashed off at the last minute. They need to be developed and critically analyzed by the key marketing executives before being submitted to top management.

7. Design and implement a program to ensure participation in the development of a marketing plan by all key members of the marketing department.

8. Develop a mentality within the marketing department that the development of a marketing plan is an ongoing and vital key to success. Many people feel threatened by marketing plans. It may be necessary to teach others that a marketing plan will help rather than hurt them.

HOW TO USE THIS WORKBOOK

This book was designed to serve as a combination guidebook and "fill-in-the-blanks" workbook. It can serve as an effective marketing plan for the next fiscal or calendar year. The following suggestions are provided to assist you in using this workbook.

1. Examine each page before writing and determine if modifications are needed to meet your needs.

2. Make necessary modifications in the forms but keep them simple and limited in number. Marketing plans often become too complex to serve as effective management tools. Don't attempt to fill the plan with details concerning tactics such as "how to hire a new salesman" or to describe the copy for a magazine advertisement.

3. Avoid shortcuts. It will be very tempting to skip Section A (Analysis of Past and Current Marketing Data) and rush into Section B (The Marketing Plan for Next Year). This would be a serious error.

4. Seek and gain approval from upper management. Superiors sometimes do not understand or appreciate the importance of a comprehensive marketing plan.

5. Provide complete information. Fill in the blank areas as completely as possible. Don't skip pages or sections of a page simply because they are

difficult or time-consuming. These may prove to be areas of vital concern to the success of the plan.

6. Substitute words that are appropriate for your company and your industry. For instance, your company may not refer to geographical areas as "regions." Use terms that are common to your environment.

7. Double-check all tables that call for numbers. Make certain that percentages add up to 100, that your arithmetic is correct, and that the numbers you use in the marketing plan conform with available reports and statistics. It is critical for all management to have confidence in your marketing plan and this necessitates accuracy.

8. Develop a personal library of other documents and reports to complement the marketing plan. Don't try to place all this material in your marketing plan. A few examples follow:

    (a) Résumés and other personal background concerning marketing employees.
    (b) Copies of magazine and newspaper advertisements used last year and during the current year.
    (c) Detailed sales reports.
    (d) Financial statements and other information such as Dun & Bradstreet reports concerning competitors, distributors, and clients.

9. Review your completed marketing plan with colleagues before submitting it to upper management. Accept helpful critiques and make changes where needed.

10. Review the plan and the workbook after completion and make necessary revisions to provide an improved marketing plan format for next year.

ANALYSIS OF PAST AND CURRENT MARKETING DATA

Before a future marketing plan can be developed, it is imperative to analyze relevant past and current marketing data. The development of a marketing plan begins with a clear understanding of "where we are."

Unless a company is undergoing a radical change, such as extreme sales growth or decline, most of the information developed in this section can be used in next year's marketing plan with only moderate modifications. Marketing plans for most organizations do not change dramatically from one year to the next.

1

Recognition of Corporate Philosophies

COMMENTARY

All successful companies have philosophies which dictate policies and procedures. In many cases, the philosophies are simply "understood" and "unstated" rather than appearing in written form. Corporate philosophies can change, and the marketing department can play an important role in helping to bring about change.

Only the most naive marketing manager will ignore corporate philosophies when developing a marketing plan.

A southeastern textile firm has an unwritten but well-understood philosophy of operating as a decentralized organization, and as being opposed to vertical integration toward the consumer. Any marketing plan which might call for greater centralization, or for entering the retail sector of the textile industry, would stand a very good chance of being rejected by management.

A west coast health service firm has an unwritten philosophy against doing business with labor unions. A marketing plan which viewed labor unions as a market target would require a very strong defense before it could hope to be approved by upper management.

The marketing department has the responsibility to explore new markets and new marketing strategies. These sometimes clash directly with corporate philosophy. A successful marketing manager will understand when it is wise to challenge corporate philosophies and when it is wise to conform. This decision depends upon a clear recognition of the philosophies which guide the company.

CORPORATE PHILOSOPHY–EXAMPLES

Singapore Airlines, an international airline, has achieved remarkable growth. This airline has stated that the achievement of the company has been the result of adherence to six corporate philosophies.

> First, we are above all a democratic organization, not in the sense of one-man-one-vote, but in the sense that we are not authoritarian, autocratic or paternalistic.

> Second, despite the size of the group, SIA strives to create the smallest possible units to carry out required tasks.

> Third, there has to be delegation of authority down the line.

> Fourth, we endeavor to create an environment in which responsibility, within the authority, can be exercised effectively at all levels.

> Fifth, training and retraining is the unwavering object of the group.

> Sixth, because of the tightly integrated nature of our operation, there is no question of one department being more important than another department. While the backroom activities may not face the same types of pressure as frontline operations, any failure is bound to have serious long-term consequences. So the acid test is utility and relevance, not relative importance.[1]

The aggressive and rapidly growing bank First Union National Bank of Charlotte, North Carolina has identified corporate philosophies as they relate to different audiences such as stockholders and employees.[2]

<u>First Union Means Performance</u>

| With Respect to Stockholders: | Consistently outperform our industry peers. |
| | Convey that we are a well managed, innovative corporation. |

---

[1] *The Pursuit of Excellence*, published by Singapore Airlines, pp. 21–22. Used with permission.
[2] First Union National of Charlotte, NC; in-house document. Used with permission.

With Respect to Customers:	Relate to customers in a courteous, friendly and personal manner.
	Deliver flexible banking services which are accurate, efficient, timely, and meet customer needs.
	Provide quality products and services which are fairly and competitively priced.
	Communicate effectively with customers.
With Respect to Employees:	Provide sufficient training to enable employees to successfully perform their work and to enhance promotional opportunities.
	Encourage open communication and support between employees at all levels.
	Create a participative environment for setting goals, seeking employee input, meeting personal objectives, and encouraging individual responsibility.
	Be an enjoyable place to work.
	Satisfy the individual needs of employees for recognition, rewards, self-esteem and personal growth.
	Provide competitive compensation and benefits commensurate with contribution.
With Respect to Community:	Conduct our business in an ethical manner.
	Provide financial support to assist in improving the quality of life.
	Encourage employee participation in community improvement activities.

USES OF CORPORATE PHILOSOPHY IN A MARKETING PLAN

Example from Singapore Airlines

Philosophy: Training and retraining is the unwavering object of the group.

Possible Application: A marketing plan for a company with that type of philosophy should include educational programs for all marketing employees. Secretaries might need to be trained in the use of word processing equipment. Senior level marketing people might need to attend conferences on strategic planning. Sales people might need training in the use of telemarketing as a tool.

Example from First Union National Bank

Philosophy: Communicate effectively with customers.

Possible Application: Effective communication with customers necessitates much more than TV advertisements and an occasional letter from the company.

Effective communication involves a well-planned program that encompasses all forms of customer communication. This might involve a training program for bank personnel who daily interface with the customer. It could also require a revamping of all point-of-purchase signs and displays in the bank. The use of Automatic Teller Machines presents a particular challenge to a bank as it requires creativity to find a way to enhance communication through a machine. The advertising and sales promotion program for a company with this philosophy would need to reflect tactics to improve customer communication. Other areas of the plan such as human resource development would also need to reflect this philosophy.

DESCRIPTION OF CORPORATE PHILOSOPHIES

A. Describe the primary corporate philosophies (written or unwritten) which may have an impact on marketing programs.

1.

2.

3.

4.

5.

6.

2

Analysis of External Environment

The level of economic activity within a market will have a direct bearing on market potential. In general, if leading economic indicators are positive, such as an increase in employment, the market potential for most goods or services will increase. While this may be true for items such as new furniture and new clothing, the reverse may be true for the sales of used furniture, used clothing, and auto parts, which may increase as economic conditions worsen.

It is essential for a marketing plan to include an analysis of economic indicators which are relevant to the products or services under consideration.

Sufficient data for purposes of developing a marketing plan are usually available without cost or at a minimal charge. Government agencies, trade associations, banks, universities, business publications, and investment houses are primary sources of information concerning economic conditions. In addition, private individuals and organizations provide newsletters and advice for a fee.

How to Interpret Economic Indicators

1. Look for trends in the data over a period of time. Trends can often be more useful than a number provided by a single economic indicator.

2. Compare and contrast several leading indicators. Look for apparent contradictions as well as indicators that reinforce one another. Remain inquisitive and ask yourself what is the probable implication and meaning of these findings.

3. Look for correlative factors between economic indicators and sales for the products/services of your industry and your company. Be careful! These may be due to coincidence rather than indicate cause and effect. Mathematical/statistical techniques exist such as "Correlation Analysis" which may assist in this area. These techniques are no longer considered particularly difficult. Someone within your organization, such as in marketing research, forecasting, or strategic planning, may be able to assist in this area. If not, the services of a consultant may be helpful. Knowledgeable persons can be found in private consulting firms and within management schools of most universities.

4. Don't use too many indicators as this can be time-consuming and confusing. Remember, marketing planners are not economists, they are searching only for tools to assist in planning.

5. Don't use economic indicators as "absolutes." All economic indicators are subject to error and are also subject to change. In many cases, unforeseen social, political, and economic events may cause the economic indicator to become invalid within a short period of time.

How to Use Economic Indicators

1. All economic indicators should be viewed solely as one piece of evidence in determining the strategies which should be incorporated into a marketing plan. Remember, two individuals with the same background and ability may interpret economic indicators entirely opposite. One may view them as indicating a worsening market and may decide to cut back all marketing activities, another may view the indicator as demonstrating opportunity and a need for intensified marketing activity.

2. In general, economic activities are viewed as tools to help determine market potential and trends in market behavior.

ECONOMIC ANALYSIS OF MARKETS SERVED BY THIS COMPANY

Primary Economic Conditions in Major Markets served by this Company	Likely to Improve		No Change Likely	Likely to Worsen	
	Substantially	Somewhat	No Change Likely	Somewhat	Substantially
_____	☐	☐	☐	☐	☐
_____	☐	☐	☐	☐	☐
_____	☐	☐	☐	☐	☐
_____	☐	☐	☐	☐	☐
_____	☐	☐	☐	☐	☐
_____	☐	☐	☐	☐	☐
_____	☐	☐	☐	☐	☐

Examples of Primary Economic Conditions: Unemployment, Teenage Employment, Bankruptcies, Inflation.

_____

_____

_____

_____

_____

_____

_____

ECONOMIC ANALYSIS

Briefly describe the probable effects during the next year of primary economic factors on (a) our markets and (b) our marketing strategies.

Primary Economic Factors That Affect Markets Served by This Company

Example: Higher mortgage rates

(a) Probable effect upon markets: As a manufacturer of brick we may see housing starts decline next year.

(b) Probable effect on marketing strategies: Place increased emphasis on the light commercial market for apartments, churches and office buildings. Start a training program for our salesmen to call on architects.

Example: Increased unemployment

(a) Probable effect on markets: As a service company in the temporary help business we may have a difficult time finding qualified and skilled labor.

(b) Probable effect on marketing strategies: Increased advertising budget to attract qualified persons interested in working part time.

Economic factor: _____

(a) Probable effect on markets:

_____
_____
_____

(b) Probable effect on marketing strategies: _____

_____
_____
_____

Economic factor: _____   (a) Probable effect on markets:

_____   _____

                                        _____

                                        _____

                                      (b) Probable effect on marketing

                                        strategies: _____

                                        _____

                                        _____

                                        _____

Economic factor: _____   (a) Probable effect on markets:

_____   _____

                                        _____

                                        _____

                                      (b) Probable effect on marketing

                                        strategies: _____

                                        _____

                                        _____

                                        _____

Economic factor: _____   (a) Probable effect on markets:

_____   _____

                                        _____

                                        _____

                                      (b) Probable effect on marketing

                                        strategies: _____

                                        _____

                                        _____

                                        _____

COMMENTARY
POLITICAL AND SOCIAL ENVIRONMENT

The success of a marketing plan is dependent on favorable political and social environments. This is particularly evident in third world countries where revolutions, riots, and other social–political disturbances often threaten marketing activities.

The effects of political and social changes in nations such as the United States and Canada are generally less severe but remain important. At the national level, political actions such as deregulation, increased taxes, and the elimination of trade barriers can have profound effects on marketing activities. Sometimes, a change in the political party in control can affect marketing plans.

At the state and local levels, political factors such as the acceptance or rejection of bond issues and urban renovation can have positive or negative marketing implications.

Social changes such as trends toward conservative or liberal life styles have both immediate and long-term marketing implications. Changes in mobility, marriage and divorce, working women, and many other societal factors may be considered in the preparation of a marketing plan. Since each marketing plan must be custom-made, only those factors which have direct influence on the products under consideration should be included.

Sources of Information on Political and Social Changes

The local newspaper, TV, and radio are primary sources. Marketing managers at all levels should keep themselves apprised of what is occurring within their geographical areas of responsibility.

In some cases, such as in the development of marketing plans for third world nations, outside consultants may be used. Normally, this is unnecessary for domestic markets.

One of the primary responsibilities of a trade association is to provide members with updated information concerning social and political trends likely to affect their industry. Private newsletters available on a subscription basis may be useful.

POLITICAL ANALYSIS OF MARKETS SERVED BY THIS COMPANY

	Likely to Improve		No Change Likely	Likely to Worsen	
Major Factors and Events Likely to Affect our Marketing Strategies	Substantially	Somewhat		Somewhat	Substantially
_____	☐	☐	☐	☐	☐
_____	☐	☐	☐	☐	☐
_____	☐	☐	☐	☐	☐
_____	☐	☐	☐	☐	☐
_____	☐	☐	☐	☐	☐
_____	☐	☐	☐	☐	☐
_____	☐	☐	☐	☐	☐

Briefly describe how these changes in economic conditions are likely to affect this marketing plan.

_____

_____

_____

_____

_____

_____

_____

POLITICAL ANALYSIS

Briefly describe the probable effects during the next year of political events on (a) our markets and (b) our marketing strategies.

Political Events Likely to Affect Our Marketing Strategies

Example: Rent Control Market A

(a) Probable effect on our markets: It is likely to create a shortage of available apartments and possibly reduce maintenance expenditures by landlords.

(b) Probable effect on our marketing strategies: As a real estate developer, this law might cause us to seek new markets. Market A might not be economically attractive next year.

Example: Deregulation

(a) Probable effect on our markets: It is likely to increase the number of competitors in the short-run, with possible price reductions and an intensified scramble for market segments.

(b) Possible effect on our marketing strategies: We might have to lower prices for some or all of our products in some or all of our markets (call our attorney to check on legality). We might have to increase our advertising budget and go after new market segments.

Political Event: _____

_____

(a) Probable effect on our markets:

_____

_____

_____

(b) Probable effect on our marketing

strategies: _____

_____

_____

_____

Political Event: _____   (a) Probable effect on our markets:

_____   _____

_____

_____

(b) Probable effect on our marketing
strategies: _____

_____

_____

_____

Political Event: _____   (a) Probable effect on our markets:

_____   _____

_____

_____

(b) Probable effect on our marketing
strategies: _____

_____

_____

_____

Political Event: _____   (a) Probable effect on our markets:

_____   _____

_____

_____

(b) Probable effect on our marketing
strategies: _____

_____

_____

_____

Political Event: _____   (a) Probable effect on our markets:

_____   _____

_____

_____

(b) Probable effect on our marketing
strategies: _____

_____

_____

_____

Political Event: _____

_____

(a) Probable effect on our markets:

_____

_____

_____

(b) Probable effect on our marketing
strategies: _____

_____

_____

_____

Political Event: _____

_____

(a) Probable effect on our markets:

_____

_____

_____

(b) Probable effect on our marketing
strategies: _____

_____

_____

_____

SOCIAL ANALYSIS OF MARKETS SERVED BY THIS COMPANY

Describe any significant social changes which are occurring within our markets that are likely to affect this marketing plan in a positive or negative manner.

1. _____

_____

_____

_____

2. _____

_____

_____

_____

3. _____

_____

_____

_____

SOCIAL ANALYSIS

Briefly describe the probable effects during the next year of changing social factors on (a) our markets and (b) our marketing strategies.

Changing Social Events Likely to Affect Our Marketing Strategies

Example: More working wives

(a) Probable effect on our markets: As a company using the "Party Plan" distribution system we will find a declining market for our products.

(b) Probable effect on our marketing strategies: We will need to develop new distribution systems such as direct mail.

Example: Larger number of retirees

(a) Probable effect on our markets: As a Southeast bank we can expect greater numbers of retirees in our market.

(b) Probable effect on our marketing strategies: We need to develop new financial products for the retiree market and find new ways to promote our services, such as sponsoring social events.

Social Change: _____

_____

(a) Probable effect on our markets:

_____

_____

_____

(b) Probable effect on our marketing strategies: _____

_____

_____

_____

Social Change: _____

_____

(a) Probable effect on our markets:

_____

_____

_____

           (b) Probable effect on our marketing
                strategies: _____

_____

_____

_____

Social Change: _____   (a) Probable effect on our markets:

_____   _____

_____

_____

           (b) Probable effect on our marketing
                strategies: _____

_____

_____

_____

Social Change: _____   (a) Probable effect on our markets:

_____   _____

_____

_____

           (b) Probable effect on our marketing
                strategies: _____

_____

_____

_____

Social Change: _____   (a) Probable effect on our markets:

_____   _____

_____

_____

           (b) Probable effect on our marketing
                strategies: _____

_____

_____

_____

Social Change: _____   (a) Probable effect on our markets:

_____   _____

                                   _____

                                   _____

                                   (b) Probable effect on our marketing
                                       strategies: _____

                                   _____

                                   _____

                                   _____

Social Change: _____   (a) Probable effect on our markets:

_____   _____

                                   _____

                                   _____

                                   (b) Probable effect on our marketing
                                       strategies: _____

                                   _____

                                   _____

                                   _____

KEEP THE ANALYSIS SIMPLE

The forms provided in this book were designed for simplicity. Considerably more information may be required in some organizations. However, most marketing managers do not need and will not use detailed or complex information pertaining to political and social conditions.

Select major political and social events that are likely to affect markets served by your company and/or are likely to affect marketing strategies. There is never a shortage of proposed laws that affect marketing. These occur at the local, state, federal, and international levels. There are also political events such as presidential or mayoral elections, which often affect markets and marketing strategies.

Astute marketing managers and staff are generally aware of social changes such as an increasing divorce rate, an increase in working women, and retirement trends. If marketing managers and staff are oblivious to important social changes, they must be required to get into the field, to attend trade shows, to read more periodicals, and possibly to develop a formalized program of staff updating. If key marketing people remain ignorant of social change, there is need for a serious review of department management and staff requirements.

The process of selecting major political and social events for discussion in a marketing plan varies among companies. Some organizations hold formal annual seminars in which outside speakers such as elected officials and professors of sociology and political science are invited to speak and answer questions.

Most organizations lack a formal procedure. In these, the decision regarding which political and social events to include in the marketing plan should be made after discussion with management trade association representatives and others who are acutely aware of changes in the political and social environment.

3

Internal Organization

A standardized organizational form does not exist. An organizational form must be designed to meet the needs of a company. This chart should show the current organizational relationship of the marketing department relative to other departments in the company. It should also show titles of individuals who head all departments.

The organizational chart should clearly show the composition of the marketing department and who reports to whom. Titles should be used on the chart.

A solid line generally depicts a direct line of authority–supervision between positions. A broken line generally indicates shared authority–supervision or an advisory relationship as opposed to a subordinate relationship.

Organizational charts are difficult to construct in some companies because the lines of authority and responsibility are not clearly defined. Sometimes top management indicates it does not believe in organizational charts.

Unless there is a company policy against the use of an organizational chart, one should be included in this plan even though it is imperfect and subject to change. It is critical to understand the organizational structure of a company. An organizational chart can be invaluable in training new employees and can help to avoid embarrassments and improve communications.

MARKETING MANAGEMENT

The terms marketing and marketing management are used daily throughout the world by all types of organizations. A simple definition seldom suffices but the author of a leading textbook has hit the nail on the head by defining marketing management as "The analysis, planning, implementation and control of programs designed to create, build, and maintain beneficial exchanges and relationships with target markets for the purpose of achieving organizational objectives."[1] Peter Drucker has gone beyond that to say that "Marketing is so basic that it cannot be considered as a separate function...It is the whole business seen from the point of view of its final result, that is, from the customer's point of view."[2]

It may be helpful to visualize marketing as an umbrella. (See Figure 3–1.) The top portion of the umbrella (the part that sheds rain) may be thought of as planning and control functions.

Planning is both strategic and operational. Strategic planning is primarily concerned with long-range issues such as the mix of products within a product portfolio. A mix of products in different stages of the life cycle is an aspect of strategic planning. Tobacco companies such as R. J. Reynolds and Philip Morris have diversified their product portfolios to include many consumer products in addition to tobacco. Cigarettes and other tobacco products may be viewed as "cash cows" that generate substantial profits, but may have a limited life cycle compared to packaged food products.

A second aspect of planning deals with operational issues. This workbook describes the process of developing an operational plan. By nature, this is short-range as compared to strategic planning.

Control is another vital function of marketing. Without control of the marketing process, the best plans are simply wastebasket fodder.

---

[1]Kotler, Philip, Fifth Edition, *Marketing Management Analysis, Planning and Control*, Prentice-Hall, Englewood Cliffs, N.J. 07632, p. 14.
[2]Ibid, p. 1.

The support spokes of the marketing umbrella are functional areas that are blended together in a marketing strategy. Advertising, packaging, pricing, marketing research, publicity, and many other marketing activities must be blended together in a mix to meet specific objectives. Since no two companies are exactly alike, the blend of these activities cannot be precisely the same for different companies.

The sales function of marketing is a part of the marketing mix. However, it is such a vital part that it should be thought of as the stem and handle of the umbrella.

An umbrella can function if one or two of its spokes break. It may not work very well but it will still continue to shed water even if the user feels several drips down the back.

If the main stem is broken, the umbrella is useless and must be repaired or discarded. Sometimes companies forget the importance of the primary stem of marketing. A sales system usually depends upon a sales force. It may also employ other means of selling such as direct mail, vending machines, or telemarketing. Many companies find that it is possible to reach a variety of market segments by using a mix of sales systems. Over time, a minor form of sales may become dominant. Many marketing professionals believe that the in-home or in-office personal computer holds the possibility of becoming an important member of the sales mix.

Sales and marketing are not synonymous. Many companies have discovered that a brilliant marketing planner has no talent as a salesperson or a sales manager. Likewise, there are many stories of top salespeople who were promoted to marketing positions only to fail miserably in this area.

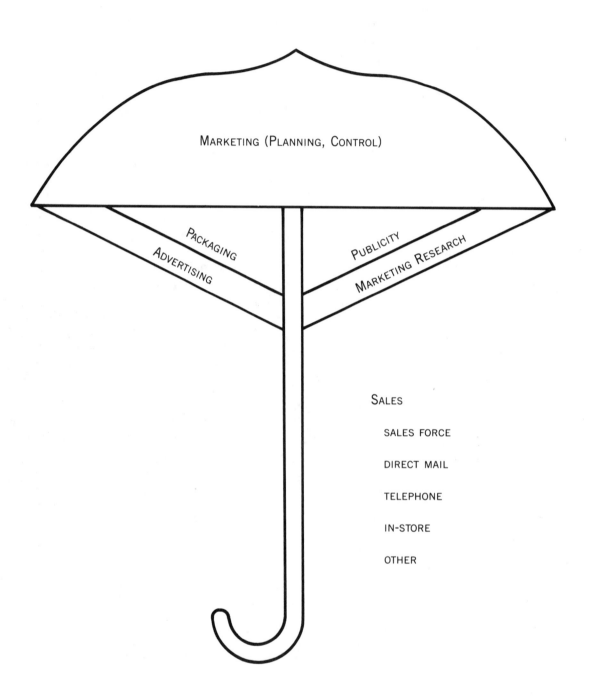

Figure 3–1

26

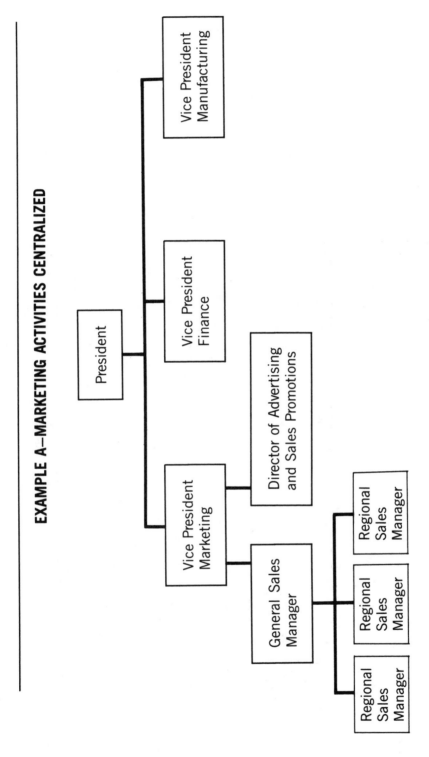

EXAMPLE A—MARKETING ACTIVITIES CENTRALIZED

This simple chart demonstrates a company in which all marketing activities are centralized under a marketing department. This form is not always possible. As companies grow, it may be impossible to centralize all marketing activities under one individual. Marketing activities may be structured by product line, by international and domestic, and along other functional means that serve the needs of the company.

EXAMPLE B—MARKETING ACTIVITIES DECENTRALIZED

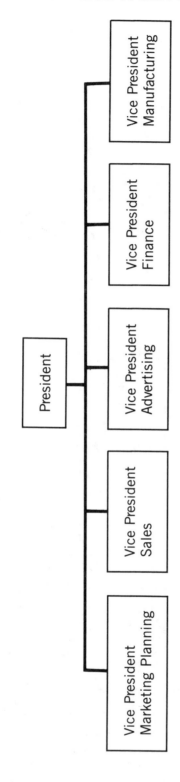

The type of organization depicted in this chart reflects a company in which the marketing concept has not been adopted. This form of organization is not consistent with creating a unified marketing approach. There may be reasons to separate marketing functions outside a single department, but generally a unified approach is preferable, and should be given serious consideration by management.

4

Competitive Analysis

COMMENTARY

A knowledge of competitors is critical in designing effective marketing strategies. It is important to understand what the competition is doing even if you believe they are wrong. This does not imply that spy-type activities are needed, nor that a disproportionate amount of time should be spent investigating or worrying about the competitor.

The bulk of information needed about your competitors is normally available if you keep your business eyes and ears open and train members of your marketing-sales department to do likewise. Several common sources of information about competitors follow.

Newspaper Articles
Articles in newspapers and business magazines.

Annual Reports
The competitor's annual report. These are available from publicly held corporations. Annual reports from privately held corporations are sometimes available through friends, relatives, and business acquaintances who own stock in the competitor's company.

Company Literature
From the competitor's literature. Very often all the information you need is available through sales information, franchise information, advertisements, public information releases, and other company publications.

Trade Shows

Through trade shows and other professional meetings.

Other Articles

Articles in trade magazines and trade newsletters.

Individuals

Salespeople who call on competitors.

Individuals who have recently left the employ of a competitor.

Individuals who are being interviewed by your company and have experience in the industry.

Published Statistics

Government and trade association reports that provide information about a particular industry.

Observation

By occasionally visiting your competitor's stores/showrooms, by acting as a prospective customer and by purchasing the products/services of your competitor.

The Competitor

Through conversations with the competitor. People like to talk about themselves and about their companies. Surprisingly, the management or members of the sales forces of competitors are often delighted to talk about their company and what they are doing even though they know they are talking with a competitor.

Other Employees

Through other employees of your company. Employees in all departments have contact with competitors and with the trade. They often learn interesting and useful marketing information.

Friends and Relatives

From friends, relatives, customers, and anyone who has contact with your competitors and is willing to share their information. Generally this is in the form of complaints or compliments about the service/products of your competitors.

YOUR SALES FORCE

Members of your sales force come into contact daily with information about competitors. They should be encouraged to write down information about competitors even if it amounts to gossip. They should also collect written information, when appropriate and possible. Customers often show salespeople contracts, sales literature, quotes and other information from competitors. This information often reflects recent changes and may indicate employment of a new competitive strategy.

Salespeople should ask for copies of the competitive information. Never allow or encourage salespeople to take competitive information without asking permission. Failure to ask for permission will create instant distrust on the part of the client and can result in a loss of credibility and business. It can also result in lawsuits.

A section of the regular sales meeting with members of the sales force should be devoted to "intelligence." This should be kept short. It is essential to keep this from becoming a gripe session in which salespeople complain that competitors offer better products at lower costs.

MARKETING RESEARCH

Professional marketing research can offer information about competitors. However, professional marketing research companies do not have pipelines of information to the deity. They obtain competitive information in a meticulous manner and from the same sources previously mentioned. The cost can often be quite high.

Consider the use of a summer intern or a part-time student assistant to gather competitive information. One of the largest chemical and pharmaceutical companies in the U.S. successfully uses this approach. Each year the agricultural chemicals division uses a team of MBA students to examine, in depth, a particular competitor. Spin-off benefits include an opportunity to see prospective employees in action prior to hiring them on a full-time basis.

Most business schools are looking for meaningful projects for undergraduate and graduate students. A competitive analysis project would be accepted by many schools throughout the U.S. and Canada.

USING COMPETITIVE INFORMATION

The task of gathering and analyzing competitive information is generally less difficult than knowing what to do with the acquired data. Managers within many industries find themselves flooded with competitive information, but seem to be baffled concerning what to do.

The following should be looked for when analyzing competitive information.

Trends — A temporary price decrease by a comeptitor may mean little. A trend of consistently lowering prices could be very meaningful. For instance, it could indicate the firm is using an experience curve production-pricing strategy and is systematically lowering prices to gain market share and achieve new economies of scale in production. Consistently lower prices could also mean the company is in deep trouble.

Look for trends and seriously question what these mean. Other competitive information such as press releases and even rumors will often indicate what these trends signify.

Variances — Variances from normal procedures often indicate a troubled competitor. They may also be signs of test markets or new strategies.

Consistency — Consistency in marketing strategies is normally verified by trends that are long-run in nature and relatively free of deviations. A consistency of competitive strategy often indicates there are market niches that have been abandoned or overlooked by a competitor.

Consistency also indicates a sureness of purpose and a solid long-range strategy that could spell trouble for your company. The IBM company seems to be a consistent competitor. It doesn't rush into markets or quickly adopt trendy strategies, but when it enters a market, previous experience indicates it will be a consistent and powerful competitor.

Shakeups in Management — Major shakeups in management are commonly followed by changes in policies and strategies. Watch for large-scale shakeups in management and anticipate change.

Financial Changes — A decline in stock prices, poor debt-to-equity ratio, lower earnings and other financial changes often precede changes in marketing strategies. Changes are most likely when negative or undesirable financial results have occurred.

Bankruptcy Threats — Competitors faced with possible bankruptcy represent opportunities for your company. Desirable marketing personnel such as members of the sales force are probably nervous and might be receptive to an inquiry concerning possible employment. Competitors faced with possible bankruptcy also make suppliers and customers very nervous. *Warning!* Members of your marketing department must refrain from telling prospects that a competitor is surely headed for bankruptcy or to add fuel to the fire. Instead, intensified promotional and sales efforts can be directed toward customers of these competitors without mentioning or alluding to problems of the competitor.

Sudden and New Success — The "new kid on the block" is often the most dangerous. Competitive Analysis should point out successes of new competitors. Federal Express, People Express Airlines, and Apple Computer found successful market niches and strategies.

It is often tempting to dismiss a new company as an upstart or a "flash in the pan" and ignore the fact that the customer is buying more of the products and services of this new company. Rather than logically and objectively examining new competition, many managers react completely with emotion. Suddenly unwise and even illegal competitive strategies are designed as a reactive response. Far too often, these embarrass the company, lead to market erosion, and to law suits and payment of damages.

COMPETITIVE ANALYSIS

Information Concerning Competitive Products

	Price	Distributor Margins	Dealer Margins	Target Markets
Competitor A _____				
Competitive Products				
A.				
B.				
C.				
D.				
E.				
Competitor B _____				
Competitive Products				
A.				
B.				
C.				
D.				
E.				
Competitor C _____				
Competitive Products				
A.				
B.				
C.				
D.				
E.				
Competitor D _____				
Competitive Products				
A.				
B.				
C.				
D.				
E.				
Competitor E _____				
Competitive Products				
A.				
B.				
C.				
D.				
E.				
Competitor F _____				
Competitive Products				
A.				
B.				
C.				
D.				
E.				

MARKETING STRATEGIES OF COMPETITORS

Product Line _____

1. Describe the current product strategies employed by primary competitors.

   Competitor A._____

   _____

   Competitor B._____

   _____

   Competitor C._____

   _____

2. Describe the current pricing strategies employed by primary competitors.

   Competitor A._____

   _____

   Competitor B._____

   _____

   Competitor C._____

   _____

3. Describe the current distribution strategies employed by primary competitor.

   Competitor A._____

   _____

   Competitor B._____

   _____

   Competitor C._____

   _____

4. Describe the current advertising strategies employed by primary competitors.

   Competitor A._____

   _____

   Competitor B._____

   _____

   Competitor C._____

   _____

5. Describe the current sales promotion strategies employed by primary competitors.

   Competitor A._____

   _____

   Competitor B._____

   _____

   Competitor C._____

   _____

EXAMPLES OF MARKETING STRATEGIES

1. Example, Product: Competitor A offers a limited line of high-quality specialty products; does not attempt to offer a broad or full line.

2. Example, Price: Competitor A offers top-of-the-line pricing. Its products are consistently priced 10–20 percent higher than others.

3. Example, Distribution: Competitor A does not use independent distributors. Company-owned minivans are used to deliver goods. Drivers are dressed in red, white, and blue uniforms with the name of the product prominently displayed. The company sells only in specialty retail stores in the Sun Belt states.

4. Example, Advertising: Competitor A does not use mass media. It relies upon slick point-of-purchase material, unusual racks and an extra 10 percent retailer margin to encourage retail support. It uses a made-in-the-U.S. theme with miniature flags on all packages.

5. Example, Sales Promotion: Competitor A sponsors 10K races in all markets. It also sponsors trips to Washington, D.C. to see the Capitol and to reinforce its red, white, and blue corporate colors and U.S. theme.

STRENGTHS AND WEAKNESSES OF COMPETITORS (DESCRIBE)

Product Line _____

	Strengths	Weaknesses
Competitor A		
Competitor B		
Competitor C		

Competitor A

Strengths

1. Heavy consumer recognition. The company has received a great deal of free publicity through its U.S.–red, white, and blue image.

2. A few highly profitable products are easy to manage and provide above-industry-average return on sales.

Weaknesses

1. Many consumers and dealers are turned off by the U.S. theme, and feel it's making patriotism a commercial commodity.

2. The company does not have a full line, and many consumers can't find products they need in this company's line. Some large retailers won't take the line for this reason.

5

Market Potential Analysis

COMMENTARY

The term Market Potential refers to the total available market as measured in dollars, units, or both, which exists for any product. Market potential is a composite of all the market segments for a product. It is a composite of the sales for all competitive products.

Determination — In most cases it is impossible to obtain a precise figure for market potential. Estimates or guesstimates of market potential normally substitute for precise figures.

Estimates of market potential may be available from trade associations, federal, state, and local governments, universities, the media, suppliers, and others who collect industrial data. In many cases, particularly with new products, dependable estimates of market potential can be obtained only through market research. Members of the company sales force may also serve as sources for estimates of market potential.

The availability of data depends on the industry and the product. Excellent government statistics exist for regulated industries, agriculture, and many others. In general, fewer statistics exist for new and unique products and services.

In some cases, the market potential for a product such as a replacement part is dependent on the market for the product which uses the replacement part. In these instances, it is sometimes necessary to estimate the possible derived demand for a product by first estimating the market for the product it serves.

Uses of Market Potential Data — Estimates of market potential assist management in determining whether or not a market has sufficient volume to serve as a viable market for the company. An analysis of market potential trends over time demonstrates the probable future size of a market and the probable rate of growth or decline in this market.

Since market potential is a composite of market segments, this information is critical to the selection of market targets. Decisions must be made concerning which of the market segments will serve as market targets. After viewing the data concerning market segments, a decision can be made concerning the market niche which a company feels it can best serve.

MARKET POTENTIAL IN INTERNATIONAL MARKETS

There are numerous examples of errors made by otherwise astute marketers who overlooked the basics when entering international markets. The glamour and excitement of entering a foreign market have caused managers to take shortcuts. Primary errors include a failure to estimate market potential, to look for market niches, and to understand the nature and complexity of the market.

Market potential in foreign markets can be estimated. Don't be fooled into believing that it is impossible or too difficult to estimate market potential abroad. This is a basic first step before entering into agreements with distributors, export agents, or others.

Sources of Information About Market Potential in Foreign Markets

Consulting and Research Firms — Most industrialized nations have professional marketing consulting and research firms. Before selecting a consulting firm:

  a. Ask for a client list.
  b. Ask for a biographical review of the professional qualifications of principals in the company.
  c. Check with reliable sources in the nation such as a branch of a bank from your country, commercial officers from the embassy, the American Chamber of Commerce, and other companies doing business in the nation.

d. Reach a clear understanding about costs, project time, and expected results. Make certain that the consultant understands what is expected.

Branches of Banks from Your Nation — Large international banks sometimes have market information that can be invaluable in examining foreign markets. In some cases detailed reports are available.

Commercial Officers — Large trading countries have commercial officers who are attached to the embassy. These individuals may have valuable information. Commercial officers also sometimes provide catalog shows for companies of the nation they represent. United States companies can get a sense of the market at little or no risk by sending catalogs and brochures for display in a catalog show. These shows may consist only of a display of catalogs in a hotel suite that is visited by local businesspeople invited by the embassy.

Government Statistics — The first place to begin looking for market potential data is in government statistics. Sometimes, data is available about foreign markets through the various branches of the U.S. government.

Most countries of the world collect data concerning their industries as well as consumption trends, population, and other demographics. These are usually available free of charge or at a slight cost. Don't accept the myth that third world nations do not have data. It is sometimes surprising to discover that considerable data is available.

Unfortunately, in some cases a foreign consultant will go no further than government offices for information, and then charge a heavy markup to the client.

Patience and personality are often the most critical factors in obtaining data from government offices.

Foreign Universities — Some foreign universities have research divisions. Like their U.S. counterparts, many have professors who conduct research or serve as consultants and can offer market insight.

Distributors — Distributors, wholesalers, brokers, and other middlemen serving markets can be helpful in assessing market potential. They should be approached in the same professional manner as their counterparts in the U.S.

Other Companies — Sometimes foreign markets are opened through a process known as "piggybacking." For example, a U.S. manufacturer of light agricultural implements might seek out an American company already established in the foreign market. This company might handle complementary products such as tractors.

Established companies from one's own nation provide logical starting points. These companies will sometimes willingly give information or market reports even though they may have no interest in handling the proposed line of products.

Retailers — A personal face-to-face survey of major retailers is often the best method for determining market potential in the case of retail products. I personally visited all the supermarket chains in Central America from Panama to Guatemala as well as managers of major hotels and hospitals. The purpose was to determine the market for breaded, frozen fish and shrimp products. In all cases, the reception was hospitable. Very useful information was obtained, including actual records of purchases for sales of frozen products.

In many markets it is unusual for retailers, institutional buyers, and others to receive inquiries from foreigners. The common reaction is to treat these people with respect and hospitality despite the fact that they may not speak the language well or may speak through an interpreter.

Journalists — This is a source that is often overlooked. Yet, all the developed nations and many of those in the third world have specialized journalists such as food or business editors.

Australian journalists were greatly helpful in an investigation of the market potential for a proposed world class resort in Queensland. Journalists can also provide excellent leads concerning others who may have market information.

MARKET POTENTIAL ESTIMATES

Geographical Markets

Product Lines	1		2		3		4		Total	
	Units	$	Units	$	Units	$	Units	$	Units	$
1.										
2.										
3.										
4.										
5.										
6.										
7.										
8.										
9.										
10.										

6

Market Share Analysis

COMMENTARY

Market share refers to the percentage of a market held by a company for a product or brand.

A market may refer to a geographical area such as Illinois or the United States. It is also common to find that markets are identified by segments such as the teenage market or the automobile "after" market.

When market share is measured, it is critical to make certain that all the data are comparable and not to include data for different markets which cannot be compared and may give misleading results. It is important to clearly define what is meant by a market such as, "the market for lightweight widgets of a certain price range within the four western states of Colorado, Montana, Nevada and Utah," as opposed to "the market for widgets in the west."

It is equally important to include only companies which actually produce competitive products in the analysis. A company that produces only bicycle tires should not be included in a listing of tire manufacturers in an analysis of the market share for tractor tires.

Estimates of market share held by competitors may be available through:

- Government trade statistics
- Independent Market Research Reports which can be purchased
- Market research studies conducted by or for your company
- Trade publications
- Estimates by experienced members of your sales force
- Information shared by members of your industry—usually available through a trade association.

ONGOING MARKET SHARE INFORMATION

A criterion commonly used to measure marketing success is the percentage of increase or decrease in market share. A decline of a few points in market share has caused highly paid marketing executives and advertising agencies to be dismissed. This is easily understood when one considers the monetary value of just one share point in many industries. A share point may be equal to one-hundred-million dollars or more.

Market share protection begins with regular and careful tracking of market share by product line and geography. New competitors seldom enter the entire market at one time. They begin by concentrating on markets in which they perceive a weakness of established competitors. Success in one geographical area enables and encourages new competitors to enter an ever-widening geographical sphere. Therefore, particular attention must be paid to market share by geographical market. Market share by product line is important, but since product line results are a composite of all geographical markets, they are slower to reflect market changes.

An optimum market share analysis will show product line market share by geographical markets. Some companies go beyond this to measure market share by consumer segment within geographical markets, and/or show market share by type of distribution channel. An example would be to measure market share for convenience stores and supermarkets within an S.M.S.A. (Standard Metropolitan Statistical Area). Additionally, it is possible to measure market share by demographic profile of customers of convenience stores or supermarkets.

The packaged food industry has private firms that sell reports of movement of goods from retail or wholesale levels. Major food processors spend millions of dollars for market research to give detailed results of trends in market share.

Many industries have become painfully aware of the importance of market share. The U.S. hotel and residential real estate-leasing industries are examples. An expansion of supply and a stagnation or slow growth in demand is a recipe for decreased occupancy and fights for existing market share among the remaining competitors. Regardless of the industry, it is critical to implement a system for determining shifts in market share on a frequent and ongoing basis.

Sources of Information

Sources of information have been previously mentioned. Customized market research is also valuable to obtain in-depth information about particular markets. If a geographical market or a product line experiences abnormal growth or decline, find out why.

Current market information is often available only through private companies. The cost of obtaining this information may seem high but lost opportunity costs are higher.

It is wasteful to purchase information that will not be used but it is unforgivable to fail to purchase information that could help prevent loss of market share or could aid management to gain additional market share.

Frogs in Hot Water — The Chairman and Chief Executive Officer of the Holiday Corporation (Holiday Inns) provided an excellent analogy in a speech presented to the second annual Hotel/Motel Development Conference:[1] "A frog, if plunged into a pot of boiling water, will either instantly jump out or perish. If the same frog is placed in a pan of cool water, it will swim about contentedly even as the temperature gradually increases. In time, the temperature will become unbearable, but by this time the frog is so accustomed to the water, and so tired from swimming within increasingly hot water, that it simply perishes without attempting to leave the pan and seek more favorable surroundings."

This is a situation that can easily confront companies which fail to regularly measure market share.

---

[1]Hotel/Motel Development Conference sponsored by Laventhal and Horwath, Dallas, Texas, January 30–31, 1986.

PRODUCT LINE MARKET SHARE

Primary Competitors (Rank)	Geographical Markets				
	1	2	3	4	5
	Estimated Market Share %	Estimated Market Share %	Estimated Market Share %	Estimated Market Share %	Estimated Market Share %
1.					
2.					
3.					
4.					
5.					
Total Market Share Competitors Percent					
Total Market Share Our Company Percent					

GEOGRAPHICAL MARKET SHARE

Primary Competitors (Rank)	Product Lines				
	1	2	3	4	5
	Estimated Market Share %	Estimated Market Share %	Estimated Market Share %	Estimated Market Share %	Estimated Market Share %
1.					
2.					
3.					
4.					
5.					
Total Market Share Competitors Percent					
Total Market Share Our Company Percent					

7

Product Line Analysis

COMMENTARY

With the acceptance and use of computers as a business tool, critical information concerning a company's product line should be readily available to marketing managers. The success of a strategic marketing plan is dependent on current knowledge of the products and product lines sold by a company. It is often true that a minority of a company's products will account for a majority of the sales.

A product line planning strategy often requires that a company's product line include groups of products of various ages and profitability levels to insure continuity.

Product line analysis is based on the careful examination of internal data. Therefore, this information must be regarded as highly confidential and the distribution should be carefully controlled. In most companies, only a few executives have access to this information. There is little reason for most salespeople to have this information, and in fact several good reasons why it can be detrimental to sales performance.

If a marketing manager does not have sufficient internal information to conduct a product line analysis as called for in this section, the development of sound marketing strategies will be next to impossible. It is essential to clearly understand your current product line before making decisions relative to the future marketing of new lines.

If this information is not currently available, it is essential to develop a system for obtaining it on a regular basis. Cooperation with other departments such as accounting and data processing (Management Information Systems) will be needed to obtain the data. In some cases, a system to obtain this data may require changes in sales forms to assist in retrieving the information. Top management must be convinced of the need to acquire and use this information on a regular basis. Increasingly, this means that product line information should not be over thirty days old.

A PRIMARY NEED

Product line analysis is basic to long-run marketing success. Unfortunately, there are examples of profitable companies in which management has little real knowledge about product lines. A southeastern textile company had never analyzed its product lines in a thorough and systematic fashion. When the task was eventually undertaken, management discovered that the sales force accounted for only one-third of actual sales. The remainder had been phoned in and neither the buyer nor salesperson knew each other. In fact, the salespeople were largely unaware that those accounts were in their territory.

This same company discovered that colors and sizes had been added but were seldom removed from the product line. The line was literally clogged with unprofitable products that overwhelmed both the sales force and the buyers. These added to inventory and production costs. Why were they in the line? What was their strategic or bottom line value? No one knew!

It is impossible to establish realistic sales objectives or quotas in the absence of a product line analysis. Many companies do, in fact, establish both without this knowledge, but are then dependent simply upon luck or a talented "feel for the market" that often disappears with age or management turnover.

Using the Data

The results of product line analysis should not be reserved solely for the development of the annual marketing plan. Instead, management and selected staff should carefully review the information on a regular basis.

Look for:

Trends — If the percentage of sales from old products increases over several months, this may be indicative of a problem with new lines or with the marketing and sales support of the new lines. New products are vital to the growth of all companies. If something is preventing that growth, find out what and take corrective action.

Sudden Changes — Sudden changes in average profit margins, the proportion of sales from new or old product lines, or sales from divisions or regions should serve as an automatic alarm. Apparently, there is a problem. Find the problem and correct it before it does serious and sometimes irreparable damage to morale, market share, and profits.

Winners — Look for winners. The effect of new sales techniques, new distribution channels, new motivational techniques, and many other variables are reflected in a careful analysis of the product line. If product lines or divisions are doing exceptionally well, make a special effort to discover why. Often the answer is surprisingly simple and might be something that could be duplicated by others and serve as a model for the company. Early recognition of winners is analogous to the discovery of gold nuggets in a stream. Chances are, there are more in that stream waiting to be found. It is critical to develop and duplicate winning techniques and products before competitors discover the stream is laden with gold.

Losers — Eventually all product lines contain losers. Products can become unprofitable for reasons beyond the control of management. The success of video game rooms was followed by an absence of customers for many in this industry. Virtually all products pass through a life cycle in which they grow, mature, and eventually decline and stabilize or die. It is the responsibility of marketing managers to recognize when products have begun to decline and to advise management that strong countermeasures are needed. These may include the sale or disposal of an entire product line.

Product Line Objectives — Each product line requires a separate annual objective. Seldom are the objectives for each new product line the same. The total of all product line objectives must equal the sales objectives for the company. Marketing managers sometimes err by applying a general objective suitable for the entire product line to each individual line. As an example, a manufacturer of electronic equipment might have five product lines with an annual sales objective of 15% increase in sales. It is doubtful that each of the five lines would have a sales increase of 15%. Instead, an older line might be expected to register an increase of only 10% and a newer line an increase of 20%. The overall objectives for a company, region, or division should be an average for the entire product line.

There are many quantitative measures that can serve as product line objectives. These depend upon your industry and your company. The most common objectives are shown on the forms that follow. These include:

Sales (Volume) — Consumer industries often use "dozens" as a measure. Others use tons, metric tons, pounds, number of people, beds, rooms, revenue, passenger miles, and many other terms. Use terms that are meaningful and common to the industry. This allows comparison to industry averages. During inflationary periods, the use of volume figures is imperative as dollar figures can be distorted by inflation.

Sales (Dollars) — The bottom line remains a monetary measure such as dollars or pesos. In periods of inflation, it is important to identify whether the objective is in constant or inflated dollars.

Margin — The definition of margin varies by industry. In some, it means the markup on cost. In others, it is a percentage of the retail price. It is well to identify, in the marketing plan, what is meant by margin and to use this same definition for all product lines.

Turn — The number of times a product "turns" is critical in some industries. Turn may be measured at wholesale or retail levels. If possible, use the same terminology for all product lines.

Market Share — As previously described, market share by product line is very important.

Other Objectives — Do not confuse slogans and philosophies with objectives. Statements such as "to be the best" or "offer a complete line" may be important company slogans or philosophies but they are not suitable as objectives. Objectives must be measurable and time specific.

PRODUCT LINE OBJECTIVES AND STRATEGIES

Describe this year's marketing objectives for current product lines.

Sales (Volume) _____	Market Share _____
Sales (Dollars) _____	Other _____
Margin _____	Other
Turn _____	

Describe this year's marketing strategies for current product lines.

Example: As a distributor of chain saws, our primary strategies for next year will be to expand our distribution by penetrating hardware stores in Missouri. We will use dealer promos and give higher discounts for volume. We will depend upon a push strategy at retail and will offer retailer training sessions.

Have the product line strategies changed during the past five years? If so, how? (Describe)

Example: We have changed our distribution strategy from complete dependence upon independent dealers to approximately a 50/50 split between chain retailers and independents. We have begun a program of dealer education and of heavy co-op advertising.

Product Strategies—Strategically Critical Product Lines

Product Lines 1. _____ , 2. _____ , 3. _____ .

Describe this year's marketing objectives for these products. Describe this year's marketing strategies for these products.

Have the marketing strategies for these products changed in the past five years? If so, how? (Describe)

PRODUCT LINE ANALYSIS—ALL PRODUCTS SOLD BY THIS COMPANY

Current Product Lines (List all)	Sales Volume Units	Sales Volume Dollars	Probable Market Share	Margin of Profit

PRODUCT LINE ANALYSIS OF OLD VS. NEW PRODUCTS

	Units	Dollars
Total Sales from New Product Lines		
Total Sales from Old Product Lines		
Total Sales from All Product Lines		
Percent of Sales from New Product Lines		
Percent of Sales from Old Product Lines		
Average Profit Margin from New Product Lines		
Average Profit Margin from Old Product Lines		
Average Profit Margin from All Product Lines		

New Product Lines = those introduced last year

Old Product Lines = those in product line prior to beginning of last year

DIVISIONS, REGIONS, TERRITORIES-SALES-CURRENT YEAR

Product Lines

Divisions	Units	Dollars	Percent of Total Sales	Ranking by Sales
A.				
B.				
C.				
D.				
E.				
Regions				
A.				
B.				
C.				
D.				
E.				
Territories				
A.				
B.				
C.				
D.				
E.				

PRODUCT LINE RANKING

	Product Lines with Highest Unit Sales Volume	Product Lines with Highest Dollar Volume Sales	Product Lines with Highest Profit Contribution
	Rank	Rank	Rank
1.			
2.			
3.			
4.			
5.			
6.			
7.			
8.			
9.			
10.			

PRODUCT LINE RANKING

	Product Lines Which Contribute Unit Sales Volume of ...		Product Lines Which Contribute Dollar Sales Volume of ...		Product Lines Which Contribute Profits of ...	
	75% of Total	50% of Total	75% of Total	50% of Total	75% of Total	50% of Total
1.						
2.						
3.						
4.						
5.						
6.						
7.						
8.						
9.						
10.						

STRATEGICALLY CRITICAL PRODUCT LINE RANKING

Rank by Importance of Product Lines

1.

2.

3.

4.

5.

6.

7.

8.

9.

10.

These products are often determined by examining information from the prior page.

8

Customer–Client Analysis

COMMENTARY

Going hand-in-hand with a product line analysis is the customer or client analysis. The information called for in this plan relative to customers is basic. It is often supplemented with detailed marketing research studies concerning customers and non-customers. If such information is available it should be included in this section.

The information required in this section of the marketing plan begins with a grouping of industries served by the company. These could be described by SIC classifications or by name such as automotive, aerospace, computer manufacturing, etc. The purpose is to identify the percentage of sales which are derived from various industries. Over time, this information should be plotted on a graph and/or shown in tabular form so that trends can be observed in a company's sales to various key industries.

A grouping of these industries according to a geographical base can also provide useful information. Any geographical grouping may be used as long as it makes sense to your company's customer base. A simple geographical grouping of North, South, East, West may be appropriate for one company whereas a more detailed one may be needed for another. Through a study of geographical groupings, sales trends can be observed. This information can then be used to reassign territories, better allocate promotional dollars, or plan other marketing activities.

A listing of all customers may be included in the marketing plan or attached as a separate report if the list is too long to be conveniently included. Frequently, this list will appear as a computer printout. A list of customers should include pertinent sales information such as the names of the customer contacts and major decision makers. Detailed information concerning the client contact and decision makers is an invaluable tool, especially to the sales manager. This information must be frequently updated to insure a base of vital information in the event that members of the sales force and/or sales managers leave the company.

An analysis of the customers who provide 50% to 75% of total sales will provide marketing managers with a list of key customers. They may require special attention in the marketing plan such as heavier service or more frequent sales calls.

Customer demographics refer to identified variables such as age and income. If possible, information about the end user should be included. This may be impossible or impractical if the company's products have widely diversified end users. Generally, this information is available only as a result of marketing research. If available, data which describes the profile of the end user can be useful in planning future marketing strategies, as the ultimate success of any product is dependent on continued purchase by the end user.

Psychographics refer to life style characteristics and are generally available only through marketing research. They are not available for many companies and many products. If this information is available, include it in this section.

CURRENT INDUSTRIAL CUSTOMERS

Demographics

Sales Performance

	Total $ Sales	Total Unit Sales	% of Total Sales from these customers	Estimated % of supplies purchased from us (Mkt. share)
Types of Industries — SIC A. B. C. D. E.				
Major Geographical Locations of Industries A. B. C. D. E.				
Names of Companies A. B. C. D. E.				
Customer Contact and Decision Makers Within Companies	Name	Address	Phone Number	Best time to visit and other information
A. B. C. D. E.				
Other Relative Information Concerning Customers A. B. C. D. E.				

INDUSTRIAL CUSTOMER RANKING BY PERCENT OF SALES

A. Customers who provide 50% or more of total sales:

    1. Number
    2. Percent of Total Customers
    3. Predominant Industries
    4. Predominant Location
    5. List all

B. Customers who provide 75% or more of total sales:

    1. Number
    2. Percent of Total Customers
    3. Predominant Industries
    4. Predominant Location
    5. List all

C. Customers who provide 75% of all sales:

    1. List all

CURRENT END USER — CONSUMER DEMOGRAPHICS

Demographics	Sales Performance		
	Total $ Sales	Total Unit Sales	Percent of Total Sales from these customers

Age

    A.
    B.
    C.
    D.
    E.

Sex

    A.
    B.

Income

    A.
    B.
    C.
    D.
    E.

Education

    A.
    B.
    C.
    D.
    E.

Race

    A.
    B.
    C.
    D.
    E.

CURRENT END USER — CONSUMER DEMOGRAPHICS

	Sales Performance		
Demographics	Total $ Sales	Total Unit Sales	Percent of Total Sales from these customers
Marital Status			
A.			
B.			
C.			
D.			
E.			
Size of Household			
A.			
B.			
C.			
D.			
E.			
Geographical Location			
A.			
B.			
C.			
D.			
E.			
Size of City			
A.			
B.			
C.			
D.			
E.			
Profession			
A.			
B.			
C.			
D.			
E.			
Other_____			
_____			
A.			
B.			
C.			
D.			
E.			

CURRENT END USER — CONSUMER PSYCHOGRAPHICS

Psychographics	Sales Performance		
	Total $ Sales	Total Unit Sales	Percent of Total Sales from these customers
Frequency of Purchase Our Product A. B. C. D. E.			
Frequency of Purchase Competitive Products A. B. C. D. E.			
Competitive Brands Purchased A. B. C. D. E.			
Method of Payment — Our Type of Products A. B. C. D. E.			
Outlets Where Our Type of Products Are Purchased A. B. C. D. E.			
Title of Person Who Purchases Our Type Product A. B. C. D. E.			

9

Pricing Analysis

COMMENTARY

Price can be one of the most effective marketing tools available to a company. Pricing strategies for a product or a product line should be established on the basis of helping to reach short- and long-term objectives. Unfortunately, prices are often established on the basis of a formula or a cost-plus basis with little regard to how these will affect the competitive position of a product or product line.

A pricing analysis is needed to provide managers with a clear perspective concerning price trends, current pricing practices within the industry, and an understanding of pricing by competitors.

After carefully studying the results of a pricing analysis, management may decide that price could serve as a stronger marketing tool. This does not necessarily imply a price reduction. In some cases, the results of the analysis may demonstrate that some or all prices could be increased to assist in meeting product line objectives.

PRICING ANALYSIS BY CHANNEL OF DISTRIBUTION

It is essential to clearly understand prices and margins at each level of the distribution system. Sometimes distributors or dealers assume larger margins over time and do not pass the savings on to the consumer. This may account for static or declining demand at the consumer level. In these cases, hard decisions must sometimes be made concerning distribution changes.

Dealers and distributors may also suffer from declining margins. If declining margins are not offset by higher sales volume, these important intermediaries may lose interest in a product line and give it less attention and less space in catalogs and showrooms.

Pricing and margin changes for dealers and distributors used by your company should be compared to competitive practices. Competitors sometimes offer higher or lower prices and margins to dealers and distributors. *Don't be confused by temporary competitive price offers.* An exceptionally low offer extended to distributors and dealers may reflect serious problems facing the competitor. Of course, there is always the chance that these changes reflect a long-term strategic change. It is the responsibility of the marketing department to continuously analyze the pricing environment and make recommendations to management concerning proper response strategies. Be careful about recommending price decreases. Sales and marketing people have established a reputation for always desiring lower prices.

PRICING OBJECTIVES AND STRATEGIES

Unfortunately, pricing objectives and strategies are often not well planned. In fact, managers sometimes express surprise at the concept of pricing strategies.

Of the four Ps of marketing (Price, Promotion, Place, and Product), price usually has the most dramatic and immediate impact upon the bottom line. Price is not simply a figure that is attached to a product at the last minute after everything else has been planned. Price is the ultimate determinant of success.

Novice entrepreneurs sometimes enter a market without studying the end price and the margins for distribution. They often learn that it is impossible to sell their product at the market price and enjoy a profit. Companies entering the retail market sometimes forget that retailers group products according to "price points." Retailers cannot offer all colors, sizes, and prices of a product. Consequently, they may offer a line of prices such as $10.95 and $13.95 retail price points. If you offer a product that must be sold at $15.95, many retailers may refuse to handle the line as it is above their price points. This may eliminate major sectors of the retail market such as mass merchandisers, and leave only specialty stores as outlets for your product.

Pricing strategies must be established so they match the kind of distribution most appropriate, the level and type of promotion possible, and the type of product being offered.

Pricing strategies have become increasingly complex in many industries. As companies seek specialized market niches and attempt to increase sales in low periods of demand, the need for multiple pricing strategies expands.

Since deregulation, airlines have offered a multitude of prices. One airline has determined that if it could find a way to change just one discount customer per flight to a full fare customer, the net effect on bottom line profits would exceed ten-million dollars per year. The stakes are high.

Successful marketing strategies depend upon well-planned pricing strategies for all product lines. In turn, successful pricing strategies depend upon careful analysis.

PRICING OBJECTIVES AND STRATEGIES

Pricing Objectives

Describe this year's pricing objectives for each product line.

Example: Product A is approximately 20% below the retail price of our major competitors. Objective: Increase retail price by 20% by end of year.

Product Line _____   Pricing Objective _____

_____

Product Line _____   Pricing Objective _____

_____

Product Line _____   Pricing Objective _____

_____

Pricing Strategies

Describe this year's pricing strategies for each product line.

Example: Increase price in two stages at six-month intervals for Product A in all markets.

Product Line _____   Pricing Strategy _____

_____

Product Line _____   Pricing Strategy _____

_____

Product Line _____   Pricing Strategy _____

_____

Describe changes in pricing strategies as compared to last year.

Example: We entered this market as the low-cost product. As our reputation has grown we have been able to command higher prices. Currently, we have a 20% lower price on most lines than our major competitors. We plan to eliminate this difference for all lines within two years and for three of our lines this year.

PRICING ANALYSIS OF PRODUCT LINES SOLD BY THIS COMPANY

Current Product Lines	Current Prices to End User	Current Dealer Prices	Current Prices to Distributors and Wholesalers	Average Annual Percentage Price Change to End User last 5 years	Average Annual Percentage Price Change to Distributor last 5 years	Average Annual Percentage Price Change to Dealer last 5 years.
1.						
2.						
3.						
4.						
5.						
6.						
7.						
8.						
9.						
10.						

PRICING ANALYSIS OF OUR PRICES VS. COMPETITORS'

Current Products (list all)	Competitive Products	Competitors' Prices to End User	Competitors' Prices to Trade
1.			
2.			
3.			
4.			
5.			
6.			
7.			
8.			
9.			
10.			

10

Channels of Distribution Analysis

COMMENTARY

The channels of distribution listed in these forms are not complete. A company may use other channels such as vending machines or direct mail. If a channel of distribution contributes sales to a company, it must be considered in this analysis regardless of the amount.

Companies often find that, over time, channels of distribution which were considered insignificant often become important to them or their competitors. As technology and costs change, a need may arise for new channels of distribution.

A marketing manager may wish to conduct a channel of distribution analysis on a product line basis and/or a geographical basis, such as the western region versus the eastern region.

It is critical to custom-design this section to fit a company's needs.

DISTRIBUTION OBJECTIVES

The importance of effective distribution is often overlooked in marketing literature and marketing seminars. Instead, companies sometimes place major emphasis on areas such as marketing research, advertising, or sales promotion. These are important factors in marketing success, but the basic secret of success in any successful marketing program is Distribution.

A company must obtain distribution strength if it is to succeed in the marketplace. Distribution strength may consist of linear feet of refrigerated space in supermarkets for a food processor such as Kraft. It might mean the numbers of salespeople in the field for Avon; franchised dealers for the Ford Motor Company; professional salespeople for I.B.M.; or numbers and quality of food brokers and distributors for a meat packer.

Distribution is and will remain the key to success in the market. Satisfaction with current distribution channels is a dangerous and often fatal mistake. A competitor is always willing and ready to find ways to take your distribution channels or to make them obsolete.

Annual distribution objectives must be established by product line and sometimes by both product line and geography. Several examples of possible distribution objectives follow.

Examples of Distribution Objectives

1. To obtain 10% additional distributors for product line A in California.
2. To reduce the total number of salaried salespeople by 25% and replace them with a commissioned sales force.
3. To eliminate the commissioned sales force for product line A and replace it with a salaried sales force.
4. To enter the convenience store market and obtain retail shelf space in 50% of the convenience stores in Virginia.
5. To establish free-standing franchised kiosks in 30% of the major shopping malls in Chicago.
6. To phase out the "party plan" form of distribution within two years and substitute a direct mail distribution system.

DISTRIBUTION STRATEGIES

Strategies are the means of attaining objectives. Many companies devote a heavy percentage of their marketing budget and effort to obtaining, holding, and insuring the success of distribution channels.

CHANNELS OF DISTRIBUTION OBJECTIVES AND STRATEGIES

Distribution Objectives

Describe this year's distribution objectives for each product line.

Example: To obtain a 20% increase in linear shelf space within supermarkets in our three-state market.

Product Line _____   Distribution Objectives _____

_____

Product Line _____   Distribution Objectives _____

_____

Distribution Strategies

Describe this year's distribution strategies for each product line.

Example: To provide a special dealer–distributor promotion involving case discounts and a travel-motivation reward.

Product Line _____   Distribution Strategies _____

_____

Product Line _____   Distribution Strategies _____

_____

Describe changes in distribution strategies as compared to last year.

Example: We have primarily concentrated on specialty stores and direct mail-catalogs. Last year was our entry year into supermarkets. We intend for supermarket sales to represent 30% of our sales by the end of next year.

ANALYSIS OF CHANNELS OF DISTRIBUTION CURRENTLY USED

Channels of Distribution	Sales Volume Number	Units	Dollars	Percent of Total Sales	Average Monthly Sales Vol. per Each
Company-owned retail outlets					
Independent retail outlets					
Sales Force — Salaried					
Sales Force — Commissioned					
Wholesalers/Distributors Company-owned					
Wholesalers/Distributors Independent					
Other Outlets					

ANALYSIS OF CHANNELS OF DISTRIBUTION CURRENTLY USED

Retail Outlets Company-Owned Stores (by name)	Sales Units	Volume Dollars	Percent of Total Sales	Ranking by Sales	Average Monthly Sales Volume
_____					
_____					
_____					
_____					
_____					
_____					
_____					
_____					
_____					
_____					
_____					
_____					
Independent Retail Outlets (by name)					
_____					
_____					
_____					
_____					
_____					
_____					
_____					
_____					
_____					

ANALYSIS OF CHANNELS OF DISTRIBUTION CURRENTLY USED

Wholesalers/Distributors (by name)	Sales Volume Units	Dollars	Percent of Total Sales	Ranking by Sales	Average Monthly Sales Volume
_____					
_____					
_____					
_____					
_____					
_____					
_____					
_____					
_____					
_____					
_____					
Other Distribution Outlets (by name)					
_____					
_____					
_____					
_____					
_____					
_____					
_____					
_____					

11

Marketing Personnel Analysis

COMMENTARY

All members of a marketing department must be considered during an analysis of marketing personnel.

This analysis begins by listing all personnel and dividing them by the geographical areas that they represent. The next step is to prepare a personnel budget form that lists the numbers of each of the various types of personnel and their dollar cost per month. Additional columns can be added to (a) describe the percentage of dollar expenditures and/or headcount that each of the classifications of personnel represents by month, and (b) the percentage of total personnel costs represented by each of the twelve months.

Non-sales personnel and members of the sales force should be treated as separate entities. The headings shown in these forms to analyze non-sales members of the marketing department such as highest degree held are only suggestions. Marketing managers should use whatever criteria are relevant to their personnel and their companies. The column headings used to describe members of the sales force, such as sales volume and ranking by sales, represent information which marketing managers need to make decisions concerning the sales force and individual members. It is suggested that these column headings not be changed. Marketing managers may wish to add additional columns.

Other information concerning the marketing personnel, such as résumés, may be included in this section. However, the sheer bulk of adding these items generally requires that they be placed in a separate notebook.

Warning! — Today, the entire area of personnel relations is filled with potential sand traps. A marketing manager's time can easily be absorbed in costly and unproductive court battles or appearances before labor boards.

Ask the personnel department for a list of pertinent federal, state, and local regulations, as well as a description of company policies and procedures. Trouble can begin with the announcement of an available position. It is critical for all managerial people in the marketing department to understand how to interview, how to appraise subordinates, and how to fire them.

Private industry has the reputation for making hardheaded, objective decisions regarding employees. Unfortunately, in some companies, this is more myth than reality. An annual objective analysis of marketing personnel is essential to insure objectivity. Organizations cannot afford to subsidize and support weak and ineffectual employees. Faced with budget cutting, this is equally true for public nonprofit organizations.

It is important to check with the personnel department and/or the legal department concerning the possibility that an employee may be given access to the written marketing plan if it contains information that directly pertains to that individual.

MARKETING PERSONNEL COUNT

This Year's Marketing Personnel Budget $_____

This Year's Marketing Personnel Headcount _____

	Numbers Total Current Year	Region 1	Region 2	Region 3
Salaried Managerial (List)				
(1)				
(2)				
(3)				
(4)				
Sales Force Salaried				
(1)				
(2)				
(3)				
(4)				
Sales Force Commission				
(1)				
(2)				
(3)				
(4)				
Office—Clerical Secretarial				
(1)				
(2)				
(3)				
(4)				
Other				
(1)				
(2)				
(3)				
(4)				
Total Personnel				

MARKETING PERSONNEL EXPENDITURES BY MONTHS

	Jan Units	Jan $'s	Feb Units	Feb $'s	Mar Units	Mar $'s	Apr Units	Apr $'s	May Units	May $'s	Jun Units	Jun $'s
Salaried Managerial (List)												
(1)												
(2)												
(3)												
(4)												
Sales Force Salaried												
(1)												
(2)												
(3)												
(4)												
Sales Force Commission												
(1)												
(2)												
(3)												
(4)												
Office–Clerical Secretarial												
(1)												
(2)												
(3)												
(4)												
Other												
(1)												
(2)												
(3)												
(4)												
Total Personnel												

MARKETING PERSONNEL EXPENDITURES BY MONTHS

	Jul Units	Jul $'s	Aug Units	Aug $'s	Sep Units	Sep $'s	Oct Units	Oct $'s	Nov Units	Nov $'s	Dec Units	Dec $'s
Salaried Managerial (List)												
(1)												
(2)												
(3)												
(4)												
Sales Force Salaried												
(1)												
(2)												
(3)												
(4)												
Sales Force Commission												
(1)												
(2)												
(3)												
(4)												
Office–Clerical Secretarial												
(1)												
(2)												
(3)												
(4)												
Other												
(1)												
(2)												
(3)												
(4)												
Total Personnel												

ANALYSIS OF NON-SALES PERSONNEL

	Number	Experience Yrs. with Company	Highest Degree Held	Sufficient in Backgrd. Ability Yes	No	Number Needed for Next Year
Managerial (1) (2) (3) (4)						
Office—Secretarial and Clerical (1) (2) (3) (4)						
Others (1) (2) (3) (4)						

ANALYSIS OF SALES FORCE

Sales Force	Sales Volume Units	Sales Volume Dollars	Percent of Total Sales	Ranking by Sales	Average Monthly Sales Volume
Sales Force Members (by name)					

ANALYSIS OF SALES FORCE

Sales Force	Years Experience w/ This Company	Education	Salary	Commission Bonus	Expenses
Sales Force Members (by name)					
_____					
_____					
_____					
_____					
_____					
_____					
_____					
_____					
_____					
_____					
_____					
_____					
_____					
_____					
_____					
_____					
_____					
_____					

MARKETING PERSONNEL EXPENDITURES ANALYSIS

Number in Sales Force   _____

Number Non-Sales Personnel   _____

Total Personnel in Marketing Dept.   _____

Dollar Expenditures for Sales Force (direct costs) $_____

Dollar Expenditures for Non-Sales Personnel $_____

Total Expenditures for Marketing Personnel $_____

Percent of Total Marketing Budget-Sales Force   _____%

Percent of Total Marketing Budget-Non-Sales Personnel   _____%

Sales Force Expenditures as Percent of Sales   _____%

Non-Sales Personnel Expenditures as Percent of Sales   _____%

POSITION DESCRIPTIONS

It is important to have a current description of the major responsibilities associated with each position in the marketing department. In some cases, these are included in the marketing plan.

In large marketing departments, the volume demands that these descriptions be placed in a separate binder.

12

Human Resource Development Analysis

COMMENTARY

Human resource development encompasses all the programs and efforts of a company to improve the skills and/or managerial talent of the employees within the marketing department. For a secretary, this might involve formal training on the use of office equipment. Training programs in salesmanship and sales management might represent human resource development programs for members of the sales force. A three-week executive program offered by a university might represent a logical program for management personnel.

Human resource development may be conducted entirely within the company, outside the company, or a combination of both.

Organizations with no plans and no budget for human resource development are probably heading for trouble. The pace of technological development in all fields demands that skills be improved and thought processes be sharpened. Desirable employees respond favorably to the opportunity to learn and may leave organizations that fail to offer opportunities for self-improvement.

Many companies now have Human Resource Departments. Virtually all mid-sized and larger companies have Personnel Departments. These are often

·charged with the responsibility of overseeing or establishing education and self-improvement programs for all employeees.

It is the responsibility of marketing management to work closely with these departments to insure that marketing personnel are provided with helpful and productive programs. The staff within human resource and personnel departments are sometimes not familiar with the needs of marketing people or the types of programs available. Consequently, they often appreciate suggestions from the marketing department. Success in this area, as with all interdepartmental relations, depends on establishing a basis of understanding and trust between the respective departments. An invitation to lunch, at the expense of the marketing department, can be an excellent investment.

Marketing people usually pride themselves on their skills in developing strong interpersonal relationships with clients. Unfortunately, these same skills are often not applied in the area of interdepartmental relationships within the organization. This has proven to be a fatal flaw to many marketing managers who found themselves without support in their own companies despite achieving success in the field.

TYPES OF MARKETING-RELATED EDUCATION—TRAINING NEEDS

Successful marketing departments hire skilled and educated people. These individuals bring technical and managerial skills with them. Unfortunately, some programs offered to marketing personnel seem to assume that these talents do not exist. It is not surprising that today's employees sometimes find training programs trite and boring.

In other cases, particularly in sales, the primary program offered to employees consists solely of motivational messages. Self-motivation, positive thinking and a solid self-image are critical to success, but today's marketing and sales employees want more depth in educational programs. Marketing and sales managers often remark that employee productivity and enthusiasm seem to improve after exposure to motivational programs, but that the effect is usually short-lived. The education-training needs of today's marketing personnel can be grouped into the following categories.

Education-Training Needs

Skills	Examples
Technical Skills	Word Processing
	Interview—Survey
	Personal Computer
	Telemarketing
	Closing—Sales

Interpersonal Skills   Client Relationships
Employer–Employee Relationships
Fellow Employee Relationships

Many skills are both technical and interpersonal. Sales skills clearly involve both. The requirements of a fast-paced, competitive, and technical society mean that technical skills soon become outdated. Interpersonal skills also need improving since it is easy to fall back on old habits or to find "generational" differences occurring. This is particularly evident in the case of "slap 'em on the back" salespeople who often find new customers and fellow employees turned off by this behavior.

Knowledge

The words "Skills and Knowledge" are used to help communicate and classify education needs. It is recognized that knowledge is inherent in skill.

Examples

Product Knowledge   Terminology; familiarity with mechanical aspects of product line; understanding of the benefits and features of the product line.

It is common to find that marketing people do not understand their product lines. This problem is not confined to technical products. A manufacturer of men's hosiery discovered that the majority of its sales force did not know the positive features of the product line and were not telling buyers about improvements in the product. Worse yet, this same sales force did not know how many colors were available.

Don't assume that all employees read or understand internal memos, sales brochures, and other information sent to them. Don't assume that all employees use the company's products. In particular, don't assume that members of the marketing department understand consumer benefits derived through product features.

The dissemination of product knowledge is not a once-a-year process. It must be continuous.

Examples

Organization Knowledge   Familiarity with organizational chart; familiarity with company policies, procedures, and philosophy.

Many marketing managers complain that they spend a disproportionate amount of time with internal problems and have little time to spend with the customer. Internal problems cannot be eliminated but they can be reduced in complexity and severity through education. Employees must be trained concerning company philosophy, policies, and procedures. It is contrary to human nature to expect all employees to thoroughly study and understand a manual. Organizations with strong corporate cultures have developed these through constant attention to employee education.

Companies in Japan and other far-eastern countries spend countless hours developing an understanding and appreciation of the organization. Singapore Airlines developed a book and even music to help reinforce the message.

Examples

Market-Environment Knowledge	Understanding of changes in markets, consumer behavior, laws.

Market conditions change. Marketing strategies must be modified or sometimes entirely changed. Management and staff positions such as marketing planning or marketing research are responsible for understanding changes in the market and the environment.

It is often useful to view these changes through the eyes of an objective outsider. Market and environmental changes often occur without full recognition by management and staff.

Some companies have found it useful to expose all members of management to annual seminars in which information is updated and a variety of topics are discussed. Individuals with knowledge about political, economic, and social changes can provide insights that later prove to be of significant value in planning. This process is particularly important to companies with multinational operations.

Examples

Managerial Improvement	Familiarity with: management by objectives, quality circles, development and use of a marketing plan.

All levels of management can grow professionally through exposure to new concepts, new philosophies, and a critical examination of old concepts and ideas. The manager who says, "I'm too busy" may soon find there is ample time, as the company or division slides into a position of irreparable damage.

Management is under attack! Competitors, the government, courts of law, unions, the family, and loyal employees increasingly confront management with new challenges. Today, management finds that subordinates, competitors, and opponents of all kinds are well-educated, articulate, and up-to-date.

"Threat" is only one reason for continuous management education and, in fact, is the weakest of reasons. The primary reason that executives actively seek new educational opportunities is for the pure thrill of learning! The human brain can be stretched. It is not a tape cassette that can absorb only a limited amount of material. There is excitement in learning!

There are no acceptable excuses for a failure to stop learning. Age, income, status, title, and responsibility are sometimes accepted as reasons that more learning is unnecessary. None are legitimate reasons.

	Examples
Self-Motivation and Personal Problems	Setting personal goals. Eliminating destructive habits. Improving family life. Personal financial management.

These are difficult times. Regardless of salary or security, employees of all companies face monumental stress and personal problems. Anyone who doubts this statement should review the latest statistics concerning divorce, suicide, drug and alcohol addiction, depression, and personal bankruptcies. Problems that affect employees off the job affect them on the job. The growth in the E.A.P. (Employees Assistance Program) is evidence that many companies have recognized the seriousness of these problems.

Your highest performing salesperson can suddenly become a zombie. Marketing research pros become burned out, bored, and quit. Secretaries become irritable and emotionally strained. Examine the alternatives. Fire the person, start over, pretend that humans are machines, or attempt to help the employee find answers to problems.

Should the cost of a personal financial consultant for employees be included in a marketing plan? Should working time be given to a spokesperson from an alcohol or drug rehabilitation program? Should your budget include a fee for pastoral counseling by a minister, priest, or rabbi? These are questions that increasingly are finding their way into marketing plans.

	Examples
General Knowledge	Current Events History Culture

Should a marketing budget include financial support for subjects that are not related to marketing? Is there any benefit to be gained from establishing or supporting educational programs that might be described as general knowledge, liberal arts or humanities? Does a newly acquired appreciation for Brahms or Bach by employees have any positive bottom-line results for a profit-making company?

There is no way to quantitatively measure the effect of general education on employees within a marketing department. Yet, if a company is multinational, shouldn't its employees be encouraged to learn a new language and the cultures of a different nation? Couldn't this result in bottom-line improvement?

This area of learning is generally the most difficult to defend in a marketing plan. It could be the most important. Men, including marketers, do not live by bread alone.

HUMAN RESOURCE DEVELOPMENT OBJECTIVES AND STRATEGIES

Objectives — Human Resource Development

A. Describe this year's Human Resource Development Objectives.

   1. Human Resource Development Objective: Example: To operationalize strategic planning and insure that all branch managers understand and are able to implement strategic planning.

   2. Human Resource Development Objective _____
_____
_____

   3. Human Resource Development Objective _____
_____
_____

Strategies — Human Resource Development

B. Describe this year's Human Resource Development Strategies.

   1. Human Resource Development Strategy: Example: To conduct an executive retreat followed by regional training sessions of one day to bring all involved up to speed on strategic planning.

   2. Human Resource Development Strategy _____
_____
_____

   3. Human Resource Development Strategy _____
_____
_____

CURRENT HUMAN RESOURCE DEVELOPMENT PROGRAM

	This Year's Expenditures	Describe
Sales Training		
Programs		
Aids		
Other		
Executive Development		
Programs		
Aids		
Other		
Non-Sales Development		
Programs		
Aids		
Other		
Other		

EFFECTIVENESS OF CURRENT HUMAN RESOURCE DEVELOPMENT PROGRAM

Value of Expenditures

	Very Worthwhile	Uncertain	Not Worthwhile	Changes Needed
Sales Training				
Program				
Aids				
Other				
Executive Development				
Programs				
Aids				
Other				
Non-Sales Development				
Programs				
Aids				
Other				
Other				

Evidence of Human Resource Development Effectiveness

1. Describe the results of any efforts to measure Human Resource Development effectiveness.

HUMAN RESOURCE DEVELOPMENT EXPENDITURES ANALYSIS

1. Current Human Resource Development as a percent of total sales. _____%

2. Current Human Resource Development as a percent of total marketing budget. _____%

3. Current Human Resource Development expenditures versus industry average. _____%

13

Marketing Research Analysis

COMMENTARY

Marketing research has become an accepted support function for marketing departments. It is no longer restricted to the largest corporations. Small and medium-sized companies can afford marketing research by contracting with qualified outside agencies or consultants.

To obtain maximum effectiveness from marketing research expenditures, objectives should be established at the beginning of the marketing plan, rather than waiting for a problem to emerge and then assigning marketing research the task of providing answers.

Marketing research can be used to provide data to support decision making in many marketing areas. A few of the more common are:

New Product Planning   Competitive Analysis
New Product Testing   Advertising Awareness
Determination of Market Potential   Consumer and Dealer Brand Awareness
Market Share Analysis   Determination of Consumer
Image Awareness   Preferences

Marketing research should be an ongoing and planned activity. The results of marketing research studies are often most useful when comparisons can be seen between the results of similar studies conducted over several periods or years. This allows marketing managers to determine trends and detect shifts in consumer preferences and market conditions. Strategies can then be implemented to match these changes.

Secondary Data

A wealth of market data is available to management through published (secondary) data. Within the industrialized world, there are many sources of published data. Federal, state, and local governments publish valuable information. Universities, trade associations, and private companies also publish statistics and reports concerning industries, products, and geographical markets.

There are trade magazines for nearly every industry. These contain stories about competitors and about industry problems and opportunities. Many companies have established libraries within their corporate offices, and maintain a staff of professional librarians. These are valuable additions to a company and should be viewed as a rich source of marketing research data.

One of the first tasks that a professional marketing research firm may undertake for a client is to search the existing literature. Millions of dollars have been spent by management for studies that were available free of charge or for a small cost. In fact, much of the preliminary task of searching secondary literature could often have been done at a substantially reduced cost by a student intern or an assistant within the company.

It is not always necessary to support a library and staff. A reading area equipped with trade magazines and statistics from various sources can suffice in most cases.

An amazing variety of directories and specialized industry reports are available at a fee from companies. As an example, it is possible to obtain a directory that indicates demographic characteristics of people by ZIP code. A company can often determine a great deal about its customers and about prospects without conducting a customized marketing research study.

Other directories classify types of company by ZIP code, number of employees, and other valuable data within geographical areas. These and other secondary information can be of great assistance in selecting market targets, deriving a prospect list, and completing many other marketing research tasks.

If your company does not subscribe to important directories and industry trade periodicals, it may be necessary to include these expenditures in the marketing research budget. There is always a good chance that the information you need has been printed and is available at a reasonable cost or free of charge. The expenditure of a few hundred dollars for directories and industry publications can save the expenditure of thousands.

MARKETING RESEARCH OBJECTIVES AND STRATEGIES

Objectives — Marketing Research

A. Describe this year's marketing research objectives for each product line.

Product Line: <u>Example: Product Line A</u> Marketing Research Objective: <u>Example: To determine consumer demographics for subsegments of the market to see if we are missing niches with our existing product line.</u>

Product Line_____ Marketing Research Objective_____

_____

Product Line_____ Marketing Research Objective_____

_____

Product Line_____ Marketing Research Objective_____

_____

Strategies — Marketing Research

B. Describe this year's marketing research strategies for each product line.

Product Line: <u>Example: Product Line A</u> Marketing Research Strategies: <u>Example: To employ the services of a professional marketing research firm to conduct a nationwide survey of users of all competitive products to product line A.</u>

Product Line_____ Marketing Research Strategies_____

_____

Product Line_____ Marketing Research Strategies_____

_____

Product Line_____ Marketing Research Strategies_____

_____

MARKETING RESEARCH PROJECTS — CURRENT YEAR

Product Research	Expenditures	Describe
(1) Current Line		
(2) New Products		
Advertising Research		
Corporate Research (Image, Logo, etc.)		
Other Research		
_____		
_____		
_____		
_____		

EFFECTIVENESS OF CURRENT YEAR'S MARKETING RESEARCH

Value as Aid in Decision Making

Product Research	Helpful	Uncertain	Not Helpful	Changes Needed
(1) Current Line				
(2) New Products				
Advertising Research				
Corporate Research (Image, Logo, etc.)				
Other Research				
_____				
_____				
_____				
_____				

MARKETING RESEARCH EXPENDITURES ANALYSIS

1. Current marketing research expenditures as a percent of total sales.   _____%

2. Current marketing research expenditures as a percent of total marketing budget.   _____%

3. Current marketing research expenditures versus industry average.   _____%

14

Advertising and Sales Promotion Analysis

Advertising and sales promotion are often placed together for planning and budgetary purposes even though the two areas are quite different.

Advertising generally refers to strategies which are employed to "pull" the customer to the company. Sales promotion generally refers to supporting strategies which are employed to motivate members of the sales force and members of the dealer–distribution network, thereby "pushing" products toward the customer. For this reason, companies sometimes place all sales promotion responsibilities under the sales department while advertising is the responsibility of the advertising department and the company's advertising agency.

To avoid using a collection of advertising and sales promotion techniques that sometimes clash with one another, it is important to establish advertising and sales promotion objectives by product line. This permits management to plan expenditures that support one another and lead toward the fulfillment of known objectives.

The lists of advertising media and types of sales promotion shown in this workbook do not include all the possible types. Managers should add those which fit their specific needs.

It is generally easier to locate qualified advertising agencies than find a "full service" sales promotion agency. By nature, sales promotion consists of a wide variety of tasks including travel incentive programs for the sales force, meeting planning, trade shows and much more. It is usually necessary to work with a variety of outside companies and specialists such as travel agencies and vendors of trade show material.

PROFESSIONAL ASSISTANCE WITH THE MARKETING PLAN

This portion of the marketing plan requires the assistance of professionals in the fields of advertising, sales promotion, and possibly public relations. It would be inappropriate for a marketing or sales manager to devote the time necessary to develop a detailed media plan.

This function is the responsibility of the advertising agency and/or advertising department of the company. These organizations employ specialists who can prepare media plans.

A marketing manager must assume responsibility for:

- Hiring professional agencies—advertising, sales promotion, public relations
- Establishing objectives and helping to set broad strategies
- Overseeing the progress of outside agencies
- Measuring the effectiveness of the campaigns (This is generally an imperfect science but must nevertheless be attempted.)

Outside professional agencies are often requested to assist in the preparation of a client's annual marketing plan. Account executives and others may attend part or all of the client's marketing planning meetings. The information called for in this section may be expanded by an outside agency, but it should never be eliminated, overlooked, or substantially reduced.

Unfortunately, not all outside agencies are adept at planning, and some do not like to provide the kinds of input called for in the following forms. Some agencies prefer to spend their time solely in the creative area. This is insufficient for the client's planning purposes. It is true that clients retain outside agencies primarily for their creative talents. However, a client has the right to expect professional assistance in planning. Budgets, media plans, and objectives must be set prior to the next year.

A great deal of advertising, sales promotion, and public relations efforts continue to be wasted or are less effective than possible. These areas cannot be allowed to stand alone. They must be tied into the overall marketing plan. This is a concept that is sometimes difficult for outside professionals to accept. Creativity is not a substitute for coordinated planning.

COMMENTARY — ADVERTISING

An analysis of current advertising expenditures will reveal the amount of dollars and the relative percentage that is spent for "push" or "pull" marketing strategies or a combination of these strategies.

A "pull" marketing strategy depends on advertising to pull the buyer to the product. Many manufacturers of consumer goods depend heavily on this strategy and mass media advertising expenditures are proportionately high.

A "push" strategy depends on middlemen to sell the product to the consumer. Those who use a push strategy usually depend on advertising in trade magazines and other media that reach the dealer or distributor. A push strategy may also involve the use of sales promotions that are designed to motivate the sales force of the manufacturers, dealers, and distributors.

An analysis of current advertising expenditures will reveal the relative percentage of advertising that is allocated for a push or pull strategy. It is not unusual to find that the proportion of dollars for push or pull is not consistent with marketing objectives.

Many firms use a combination of push and pull advertising. In the absence of an analysis of advertising and sales promotion expenditures, it is easy for the mix to become unbalanced.

ADVERTISING OBJECTIVES AND STRATEGIES

A. Describe this year's advertising objectives for each product line.

1. Product line_____ Advertising Objectives_____
_____
_____

2. Product line_____ Advertising Objectives_____
_____
_____

3. Product line_____ Advertising Objectives_____
_____
_____

B. Describe this year's advertising strategies for each product line.

1. Product line_____ Advertising Strategies_____
_____
_____

2. Product Line_____ Advertising Strategies_____
_____
_____

3. Product Line_____ Advertising Strategies_____
_____
_____

ADVERTISING MEDIA MIX — CURRENT YEAR

Media	Annual $ Expenditures	Frequency	Ad Size
Print			
Newspaper			
(1) _____			
(2) _____			
(3) _____			
Consumer Magazine			
(1) _____			
(2) _____			
(3) _____			
Trade Publication			
(1) _____			
(2) _____			
(3) _____			
Other			
(1) _____			
(2) _____			
(3) _____			
Radio			
AM (1) _____			
(2) _____			
(3) _____			
FM (1) _____			
(2) _____			
(3) _____			
Television			
(1) _____			
(2) _____			
(3) _____			
Specialty			
(1) _____			
(2) _____			
(3) _____			
Direct Mail			
(1) _____			
(2) _____			
(3) _____			
Point of Purchase			
(1) _____			
(2) _____			
(3) _____			
Co-op			
(1) _____			
(2) _____			
(3) _____			
Other			
(1) _____			
(2) _____			
(3) _____			

ADVERTISING EXPENDITURES BY MONTH BY MEDIA

Media	Jan $'s	Feb $'s	Mar $'s	Apr $'s	May $'s	Jun $'s
Print						
Newspaper						
(1) _____						
(2) _____						
(3) _____						
Consumer Magazine						
(1) _____						
(2) _____						
(3) _____						
Trade Publication						
(1) _____						
(2) _____						
(3) _____						
Radio						
AM (1) _____						
(2) _____						
(3) _____						
FM (1) _____						
(2) _____						
(3) _____						
Television						
(1) _____						
(2) _____						
(3) _____						
Specialty						
(1) _____						
(2) _____						
(3) _____						
Direct Mail						
(1) _____						
(2) _____						
(3) _____						
Point of Purchase						
(1) _____						
(2) _____						
(3) _____						
Co-op						
(1) _____						
(2) _____						
(3) _____						
Other						
(1) _____						
(2) _____						
(3) _____						

ADVERTISING EXPENDITURES BY MONTH BY MEDIA

Media	Jul $'s		Aug $'s		Sep $'s		Oct $'s		Nov $'s		Dec $'s		Total Year
Print													
Newspaper													
(1) _____													
(2) _____													
(3) _____													
Consumer													
Magazine													
(1) _____													
(2) _____													
(3) _____													
Trade Publication													
(1) _____													
(2) _____													
(3) _____													
Radio													
AM (1) _____													
(2) _____													
(3) _____													
FM (1) _____													
(2) _____													
(3) _____													
Television													
(1) _____													
(2) _____													
(3) _____													
Specialty													
(1) _____													
(2) _____													
(3) _____													
Direct Mail													
(1) _____													
(2) _____													
(3) _____													
Point of Purchase													
(1) _____													
(2) _____													
(3) _____													
Co-op													
(1) _____													
(2) _____													
(3) _____													
Other													
(1) _____													
(2) _____													
(3) _____													

ADVERTISING AGENCY INFORMATION

Current Advertising Agency

Product Lines for which Ad Agency has responsibility

In-house Agency_____

_____

Outside Agency_____

_____

Address

Phone Number

Telex or Cable

Account Executive

Describe responsibility of advertising agency_____

_____

_____

Compensation system for advertising agency_____

_____

_____

ADVERTISING EXPENDITURES ANALYSIS

1. Advertising expenditures as a percent of total sales. _____%

2. Advertising expenditures as a percent of total marketing budget. _____%

3. Current advertising expenditures versus industry average. _____%

Evidence of Effectiveness of Current Year's Advertising

1. Describe the results of any efforts to measure advertising effectiveness.

_____

_____

_____

_____

_____

_____

_____

_____

_____

_____

_____

COMMENTARY — SALES PROMOTION

Sales promotion expenditures are generally for the purpose of motivating members of the sales force for the manufacturers, distributors, and dealers. These consist of a wide variety of incentives and programs. Sales promotion is vital to the success of a "push" marketing strategy. It may also be needed to complement a strong "pull" strategy.

A complete list of all possible sales promotion tools would require a book at least the size of this workbook. Consequently, it is preferable to place sales promotion items into major categories. Additions to the following list should be made by marketing managers to match their individual situations.

Sales promotion programs should have a recognizable theme. This theme might tie into a national or international event such as the Olympics. It might also support a well-known consumer advertising theme by the same company. Another common theme is to tie the sales promotion into well-known product attributes and into associated characters or personalities.

Example: A sales promotion company designed a sales promotion campaign for a brand of canned spinach. The Popeye cartoon character was used in the promotion. This campaign was directed to the end consumer and yet was called sales promotion. This is an example of the use of the term in consumer as well as trade promotion.

The Popeye sales promotion for spinach included the use of coupons. These provided the consumer with "cents off" on two cans of spinach. An additional coupon was included for a free Popeye sticker and coloring book with crayons. To obtain this package, the consumer needed to send two labels from the spinach cans along with fifty cents for mailing.

Sales promotion campaigns directed to the trade are sometimes supported by motivational contests such as a free week in Hawaii. There are specialized travel motivation companies that assist clients in developing travel promotion programs. These companies make all the travel arrangements and may also build a motivation program including flyers, posters, letters, videotapes, and a variety of other means of getting the message to the trade. These same companies work with clients to increase productivity of salespeople, production workers, and other employees.

Compensation — Sales promotion companies are generally compensated on a fee basis. Travel motivation companies usually work on a fee basis plus commissions obtained from performing the services of a travel agent.

Locating a Sales Promotion Company

Some advertising agencies have separate divisions that work exclusively in the area of sales promotion. If you are happy with your advertising agency, this is a good place to begin looking for a sales promotion firm. The ad agency may also be able to recommend a professional sales management firm.

Look for creative sales promotion programs. These are easy to find as dealers, distributors, and members of your sales force frequently come in contact with them. Keep your eye open for good sales promotion campaigns in noncompeting industries. If you like these programs, find out which agency prepared them. An aggressive agency will be delighted to demonstrate its prior campaigns and give references.

Public Relations

The term public relations is sometimes confused with sales promotion. A public relations firm may also do sales promotions but this is not always the case. A professional public relations firm can be invaluable in obtaining public exposure for a company. In some cases, a public relations firm may also offer consulting assistance.

It is important to check the credentials, the client list, and the experience of a public relations firm. Many individuals in this field came from journalism backgrounds in which they worked with newspapers, radio, TV, or magazines. Many good public relations firms consist of only one person, yet may be highly professional in a particular area.

Unfortunately, some public relations firms offer marketing services in areas in which they have little expertise such as marketing research or strategic planning. It is the client's responsibility to check the background of all marketing professionals before retaining them for professional assistance.

SALES PROMOTION OBJECTIVES AND STRATEGIES

Objectives — Sales Promotion

A. Describe this year's Sales Promotion Objectives for each product line.

1. Product line_____ Sales Promotion Objective_____
   _____
   _____

2. Product line_____ Sales Promotion Objective_____
   _____
   _____

3. Product line_____ Sales Promotion Objective_____
   _____
   _____

Strategies — Sales Promotion

B. Describe this year's Sales Promotion Strategies for each product line.

1. Product Line_____ Sales Promotion Strategies_____
   _____
   _____

2. Product Line_____ Sales Promotion Strategies_____
   _____
   _____

3. Product Line_____ Sales Promotion Strategies_____
   _____
   _____

SALES PROMOTION EXPENDITURES BY ITEMS BY MONTH

This Year's Sales Promotion Budget $_____

Types of Sales
Promotion

	Jan $'s	Feb $'s	Mar $'s	Apr $'s	May $'s	Jun $'s
Trade Promos to Dealers and Distributors						
Trade Shows						
Sales Force Promotion						
Other Sales Promotion						
Totals (Must Equal Sales Promotion Budget)						

SALES PROMOTION EXPENDITURES BY ITEMS BY MONTH

This Year's Sales Promotion Budget $_____

Types of Sales
Promotion

	Jul $'s	Aug $'s	Sep $'s	Oct $'s	Nov $'s	Dec $'s	Year $ Total	Percent of SP Budget
Trade Promos to Dealers and Distributors								
Trade Shows								
Sales Force Promotion								
Other Sales Promotion								
Totals (Must Equal Sales Promotion Budget)								

SALES PROMOTION EXPENDITURES ANALYSIS

1. Sales promotion as a percent of total sales. _____%

2. Sales promotion as a percent of total marketing budget. _____%

3. Sales promotion expenditures versus industry average. _____%

Evidence of Effectiveness of Current Year's Sales Promotion

1. Describe the results of any efforts to measure sales promotion effectiveness.

Description of Sales Promotion Programs for Current Year
(briefly describe)

_____

_____

_____

_____

_____

_____

MARKETING PLAN FOR NEXT YEAR

This section represents the marketing plan which will be developed for use in the coming fiscal or calendar year. Much of the data in this plan will be taken from the previous marketing analysis. In most cases, it will be necessary to change the figures, such as the size of the sales force or level of advertising expenditures to meet the new objectives for the coming year.

The marketing strategies selected for next year to accomplish these objectives will determine the quantity and quality of expenditures which will be reflected in the marketing plan.

15

Sales Projections

COMMENTARY

This section does not attempt to provide a form which may be modified and completed.

There are many techniques for projecting sales, ranging from complex ones that necessitate the use of statistics and a computer, to simple guesstimates.

Regardless of the technique used, it is mandatory that a marketing plan include estimates of the possible sales for each of the product lines and each of the geographical territories served by a company. Many companies use the sales estimates as sales objectives for the next year.

Sales objectives do not have to correspond precisely to sales estimates. A marketing manager may believe that his/her company is incapable of reaching projected sales for a number of reasons.

Other managers may feel that the estimates are not high enough and that their organization can produce sales well in excess of the projections.

If your organization lacks expertise in sales forecasting, the expenditure of funds for an experienced consultant to establish a practical and usable system should be considered. A brief description of some of the more commonly used techniques in projecting sales follows.

Methods Using Historical Data

Least Squares Analysis — This is also known as two variable linear regression analysis. This system essentially draws a straight line through a series of historical data, indicating the average rate of increase or decrease in sales. The two variables are sales and time. This system is commonly used and is relatively easy to use and understand. Projections made using this system assume that future sales will not vary greatly from the average of past sales.

Other Methods Using Historical Data — It is possible to use more sophisticated techniques that do not depend on a straight line projection but instead use a curvilinear projection. However, the basis will be past data.

X Percent Increase/Year — A common method of projecting is to multiply last year's sales by X percent. Managers often pull the X percent figure "out of the air" or use a percentage representing estimated growth in the GNP or some other measure of economic activity, such as that supplied by a trade association. Although this system is filled with pitfalls, many marketing managers have used it for many years.

Methods That Measure Outside Economic Variables

Methods such as econometric models are generally too complex, expensive, and time-consuming for most marketing managers to use. Some use multiple regression which attempts to show the influence of more than one variable but, again, most marketing managers are not highly experienced in statistical analysis and prefer to use simpler techniques.

Marketing research studies are sometimes used to project customer attitudes and opinions. While these are useful tools and should be used when available, they seldom serve by themselves as a sales projection.

Sales Force and Management Opinions

Members of the sales force are commonly asked to provide sales projections without modification by management. Management should use all available tools to arrive at an estimate of sales for the next year.

Five-Year Review

Regardless of the methods employed to derive a sales projection, the use of historical data can provide a marketing manager with an idea of trends. It is suggested that information be gathered and used for the past five years. A marketing manager may elect to use more or less years. This information can then be plotted on a chart and/or it can be displayed in tabular form using the actual numbers for each of the five years.

SALES PROJECTIONS — ALL PRODUCT LINES

1. Provide five-year numerical review of sales for each product line.

2. Provide five-year trend line of sales for each product line. Show forecasted sales for next year based on trend line projections (example: Least Squares Analysis).

3. Provide five-year numerical review of profits or margins for each product line.

4. Provide five-year trend line of profits or margins for each product line. Show forecasted profits for next year based on trend line projections. (example: Least Squares Analysis).

SALES PROJECTIONS BY GEOGRAPHY (DIVISION, REGION, TERRITORY)

1. Provide five-year numerical review of sales for each product line by geographical area (division, region, territory).

2. Provide five-year trend line of sales for each product line by geographical area. Show forecasted sales for next year based on trend line projections.

3. Provide five-year numerical review of profits or margins for each product line by geographical area.

4. Provide five-year trend line of profits or margins for each product line by geographical area. Show forecasted profits or margins for next year based on trend line projections.

16

Target Markets

COMMENTARY

Today it is impossible for a company to be all things to all people. Instead, marketing managers have the responsibility of selecting market segments which represent the most likely customers for the products and services of their companies. Customers within these market segments will share certain common characteristics. The manager should develop a customer profile of target market segments which shows common demographic characteristics such as age, income, race, and other elements. Other profile characteristics known as psychographic (life style) variables can be equally useful. Both the demographic and psychographic characteristics assist managers in marketing strategies such as directing the sales force toward desired prospects and selecting advertising media which reach these prospects.

Profiles of target markets can and should be developed for industrial and consumer groups. Companies who have little or no contact with the final user may find it sufficient to develop and use target market profiles only for their industrial customers. Others may find it essential to target both the intermediary industrial customer and the end user.

Demographic and psychographic profile characteristics of target markets are determined primarily through marketing surveys, published studies, and feedback from the sales force. An ongoing system should be implemented to provide information concerning the various segments of the market served by a company so that decisions can be made relative to which segments will serve as target markets.

THE FOCUS OF MARKETING

The only acceptable focus for marketing is the consumer. Yes, marketing must be aware of production capabilities and efficiencies but marketing cannot be production driven. It must be consumer driven.

The pork and poultry industries of the United States offer examples of each. The poultry industry learned to provide a product that met the needs of contemporary consumers. Poultry achieved an image as a healthful, tasty, convenient, easy-to-prepare, fun-to-eat, inexpensive product for the mass consumer market. Consumers can purchase chicken in a variety of forms and in hundreds of locations ranging from a lunch counter to multinational franchised chains.

The pork industry has not enjoyed the success of poultry. Part of the answer may lie in the fact that pork appears to be a production-driven product. There are examples of highly effective marketing: consumer-driven companies within the pork industry that provide specialty products such as whole hog sausage or sugar cured country hams. However, as an industry, pork seems to be production driven.

A consumer-driven company is also marketing driven. It continuously seeks new ways to satisfy consumer needs at a profit. It is not limited by those who state "you can't change things in this industry" or "this is the way we have always done it" or "production capabilities just don't match what you claim the consumer wants."

A consumer-driven company cannot afford to limit its marketing activities and interests to middlemen. Many companies do not produce products that are directly purchased by the consumer. Brick manufacturers do not sell a high volume of their product directly to homeowners, but instead sell to contractors. This in no way excuses them from understanding the needs of consumers or developing new products to meet changing markets. Brick is in competition with other siding materials. If consumer preferences change, brick companies must close their kilns.

Companies that produce consumer products often sell through distributors, brokers, or wholesalers, and view these as their customers. They are wrong!

Competitors find ways to work with middlemen to push additional millions of dollars of their products into and through retail stores. Competitors also find ways to talk directly with the consumer and to pull their products through distributors and wholesalers whether or not these middlemen like the company and its sales force.

Production-driven companies characteristically produce a product and then give it to the sales department to sell. We produce and you sell! You perform your function and we'll perform ours. Leave us alone and we won't bother you; just get out there and sell those products. Companies with this mentality may rename the sales department and call it marketing. A mountain may be called a lake but it remains a mountain.

Marketing begins and ends with the consumer. Fulfillment of consumer needs is the ultimate purpose of marketing. Products can be *sold* to consumers only as long as competitors have not found ways to fulfill consumer needs. Imagine what marketing could do for the Soviet economy if it were allowed to exist.

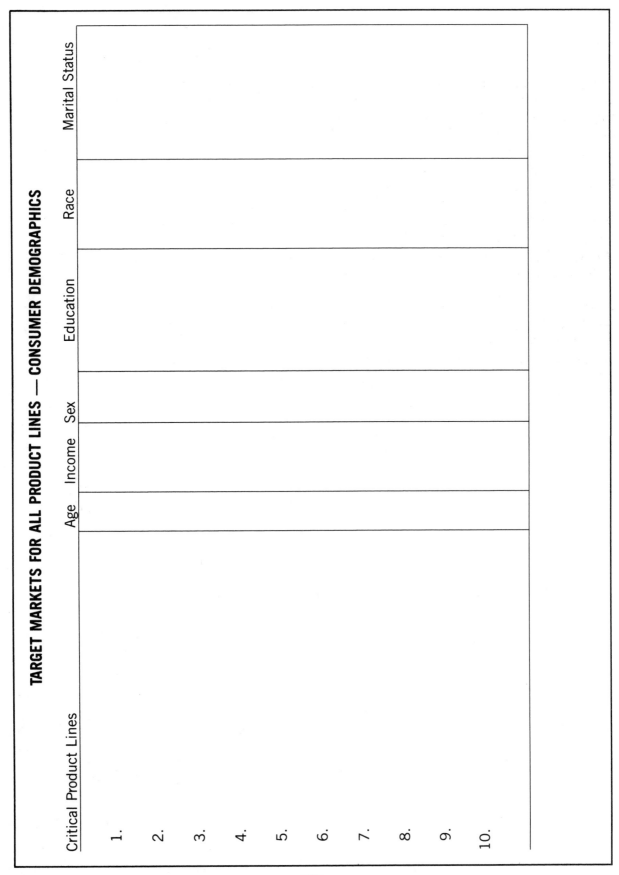

TARGET MARKETS FOR ALL PRODUCT LINES — CONSUMER DEMOGRAPHICS

Critical Product Lines

Age   Income   Sex   Education   Race   Marital Status

1.

2.

3.

4.

5.

6.

7.

8.

9.

10.

131

TARGET MARKETS FOR STRATEGICALLY CRITICAL PRODUCT LINES — CONSUMER DEMOGRAPHICS

Product Lines	Household Size	Geographical Location	Size of City	Profession	Other	Other	Other
1.							
2.							
3.							
4.							
5.							
6.							
7.							
8.							
9.							
10.							

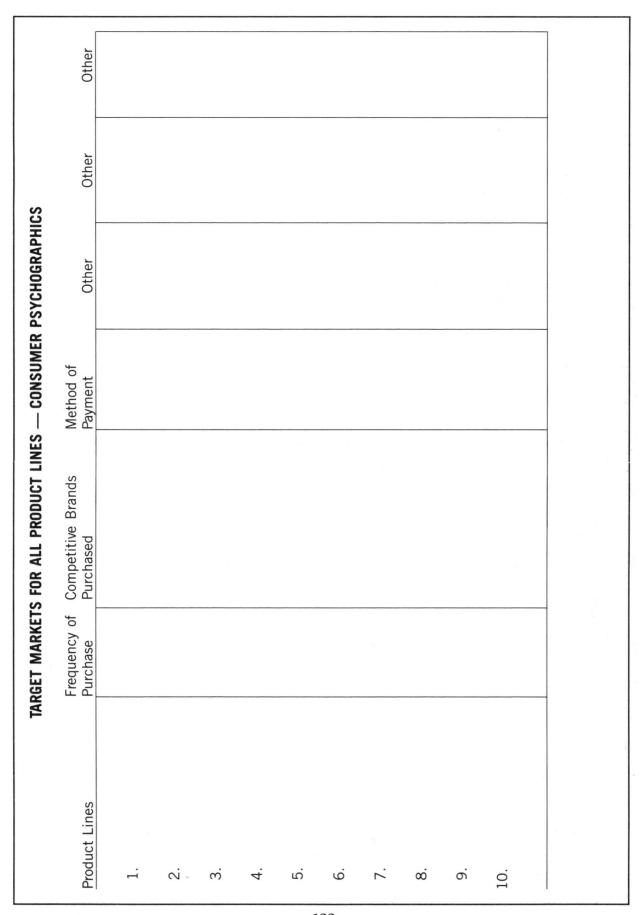

TARGET MARKETS FOR ALL PRODUCT LINES — CONSUMER PSYCHOGRAPHICS

Product Lines	Frequency of Purchase	Competitive Brands Purchased	Method of Payment	Other	Other	Other
1.						
2.						
3.						
4.						
5.						
6.						
7.						
8.						
9.						
10.						

TARGET MARKETS FOR ALL PRODUCT LINES — INDUSTRIAL DEMOGRAPHICS

Product Lines	Type of Industry	Types of Companies	Geographical Locations	Size of Company	Other	Other	Other	Decision Maker Within Companies
1.								
2.								
3.								
4.								
5.								
6.								
7.								
8.								
9.								
10.								

17

Marketing and Sales Objectives

COMMENTARY

Marketing objectives should be established so that they help the company to achieve its goals. A company might have a goal of reaching sales of $600 million by the end of a five-year period. Marketing then has the responsibility to insure that this goal is reached.

This is done by establishing marketing objectives. To insure that marketing objectives are met, each of the component areas of marketing such as Sales, Advertising, and others must have objectives which directly work toward fulfillment of the marketing objectives.

Objectives should be broken down so that each sales area, each salesperson, and each product line have objectives which must be met. The purpose for these subobjectives is to insure that major marketing objectives are met.

An objective must be time-specific. It must also be quantity-specific. An example would be: "to obtain sales of $50,000 per week for product A by December of next year."

Sometimes objectives and slogans are confused. A statement such as "to be the best," or "to serve our customers well" are slogans. They are not objectives and should never be substituted for an objective.

Objectives must be stated in such a way that results can be measured so that everyone can easily determine whether objectives were met.

Marketing objectives generally are stated in terms such as achieving X percent market share for a particular product line or lines, achieving X percent market penetration within certain market segments with selective products, and achieving X percent sales growth for all or selected product lines. It is common for marketing objectives to be accompanied with a statement concerning cost and/or profitability such as "to increase market penetration by X percent for product A in the Chicago market at a profit of X percent."

Marketing and sales objectives require considerable thought and time to construct. They cannot be hastily drawn up at the last minute. Marketing objectives should give direction to all areas of the marketing department for the next year. They should be directly used to set quotas, establish bonuses, and determine the kinds of personnel needed in all areas.

MARKETING OBJECTIVES

Describe the marketing objectives for next year for all product lines.

Product Line _____A_____

Objective Example: To increase total unit sales within the Northeast by 12 percent, within the Southeast by 16 percent, and to initiate market entry in the Midwest and achieve at least a 5 percent market share by the end of the year.

Product Line _____

Objective _____

_____

_____

Product Line _____

Objective _____

_____

_____

SALES OBJECTIVES FOR ALL PRODUCT LINES

Percent of Sales from Existing Product Lines   _____

Percent of Sales from New Product Lines   _____

Percent of Sales from Strategically Critical Product Lines   _____

Average Profit Margin for New Product Lines   _____

Average Profit Margin for Existing Product Lines   _____

Average Profit Margin for All Product Lines   _____

SALES OBJECTIVES FOR STRATEGICALLY CRITICAL PRODUCT LINES

Rank by Importance All Strategically
Critical Product Lines

	Units	Dollars	Market Share	Profit Margin
1.				
2.				
3.				
4.				
5.				
6.				
7.				
8.				
9.				
10.				

SALES OBJECTIVES FOR ALL DISTRIBUTION CHANNELS

	Annual Sales Units - Dollars		Average Monthly Sales Units - Dollars		Number of Outlets Needed
Total Sales from New Distribution Channels					
Total Sales from Current Distribution Channels					
Total Sales from All Distribution Channels (This must equal sales objectives)					

SALES OBJECTIVES FOR ALL DISTRIBUTION CHANNELS

Units _____ Dollars _____

Distribution Channels	Annual Sales Units - Dollars		Average Monthly Sales Units - Dollars		Number of New Outlets Needed
Retail Stores — Company-owned (list locations)					
Independent Stores (list locations)					
Wholesalers/Distributors (list locations)					
Other Distribution Channels (list type and location)					

SALES OBJECTIVES FOR DISTRIBUTION CHANNELS BY MONTH

Distribution Channels	Jan Units	$'s	Feb Units	$'s	Mar Units	$'s	Apr Units	$'s	May Units	$'s	Jun Units	$'s
Retail Stores — Company-owned (list locations)												
Independent Stores (list locations)												
Wholesalers/Distributors (list locations)												
Other Distribution Channels (list type and location)												

SALES OBJECTIVES FOR DISTRIBUTION CHANNELS BY MONTH

Distribution Channels	Jul Units	$'s	Aug Units	$'s	Sep Units	$'s	Oct Units	$'s	Nov Units	$'s	Dec Units	$'s
Retail Stores — Company-owned (list locations)												
Independent Stores (list locations)												
Wholesalers/Distributors (list locations)												
Other Distribution Channels (list type and location)												

SALES OBJECTIVES FOR SALES FORCE

Region	Annual Sales Objectives Units	Dollars	Monthly Sales Objectives Units	Dollars
Existing Sales Force Members (by name)				
_____				
_____				
_____				
_____				
_____				
_____				
_____				
Total Sales Expected from Existing Sales Force				
_____				
New Sales Force Members (numbers needed)				
_____				
_____				
_____				
_____				
_____				
_____				
_____				
Total Sales Expected from New Members of Sales Force				
Total Sales Expected from All Members of Sales Force				

144

SALES OBJECTIVES FOR SALES FORCE BY MONTH

Members of Sales Force	Jan Units	$'s	Feb Units	$'s	Mar Units	$'s	Apr Units	$'s	May Units	$'s	Jun Units	$'s
1.												
2.												
3.												
4.												
5.												
6.												
7.												
8.												
9.												
10.												

SALES OBJECTIVES FOR SALES FORCE BY MONTH

Members of Sales Force	Jul Units	$'s	Aug Units	$'s	Sep Units	$'s	Oct Units	$'s	Nov Units	$'s	Dec Units	$'s
1.												
2.												
3.												
4.												
5.												
6.												
7.												
8.												
9.												
10.												

18

Marketing Strategies

COMMENTARY

Marketing strategies are designed to accomplish marketing objectives. Strategies are built using a mixture of the "four Ps." Product-Package, Price, Promotion (advertising) and Place (distribution) represent the "four Ps."

Marketing strategies vary from company to company, product line to product line, and year to year. Marketing strategies must be responsive to market conditions and to objectives. Thus, a strategy which produced excellent results this year may be a failure next year.

Strategies must be designed to meet competitive moves. They must also be designed to provide a profit objective within budget constraints.

A limited number of well-designed marketing strategies should be written to guide the department in its marketing activities for the next year. In the absence of well-defined and logical marketing strategies presented in a written form, marketing efforts will almost assuredly become fragmented and take on the appearance of "putting out brush fires."

Once a series of general marketing strategies has been agreed to, it is necessary to develop subobjectives and strategies for each of the areas within the marketing department such as sales, advertising, and marketing research to support the primary objectives and strategies for the department.

Example: "To accomplish the objective of achieving 10 percent additional sales by the end of next year in the southeast region for Product A: Medium-size textile manufacturers will be selected as the target market. A new, lighter model of Product A will be offered since it matches the needs of these manufacturers. Prospects will be reached through a combination of our direct sales force and independent distributors. Promotional support will occur through trade magazines and direct mail. To help insure initial purchases, a series of price discounts will be given for orders of various quantities for the first 60 days of the year."

Managers of areas such as sales and advertising must then use this strategy as a guideline when planning and implementing the details such as the number of new salespeople needed, the names of trade magazines to use, and the type of message to be presented in advertisements.

DESIGNING PRODUCT LINES

In some companies, management has never officially recognized the existence of separate product lines. This is often a mistake. Product line objectives and strategies cannot be established if product lines do not exist. In short, the basis for establishing a meaningful marketing plan does not exist in these cases.

Product lines are commonly established by placing products into natural groups. Criteria commonly used to design product lines include the following:

- They serve the same market segments.
- They are sold through the same channels of distribution; example: Police Forces, Vending Machines, Furniture Stores.
- They are sold in the same geographical markets.
- They are manufactured by a common process or from a common substance.

In a marketing-driven economy, it makes sense to design product lines according to common market segments and/or common channels of distribution. Other means of designing product lines may satisfy existing accounting procedures or manufacturing processes, but these often do not lend themselves to a marketing orientation. This creates confusion in marketing planning and may interfere with achieving efficiencies in that area.

The evidence from highly successful marketing-oriented companies strongly indicates there are definite advantages in grouping products into product lines. It is also apparent that groupings sometimes need to be changed. Conditions within the marketplace may dictate that the current grouping of products into certain product lines needs to be seriously reviewed. Normally, the most difficult hurdle to overcome in reviewing and restructuring product lines is internal politics. Someone will always be threatened by a restructuring of product lines.

Product lines are commonly managed by a product line manager. Individual brands may be important enough to demand brand managers. This concept is sometimes difficult for top management to embrace, particularly within companies that are led by the entrepreneur founder. Marketing managers who suggest this system may be accused of empire building and of desiring an expensive bureaucracy. Again, the evidence from highly successful companies within the product and service sectors and within both the industrial and consumer goods areas strongly suggests that a system of product line management is essential for growth. Eventually, there is an absolute limit to the number of different brands or products that any one person can effectively manage, even with the aid of a computer.

STRATEGICALLY CRITICAL PRODUCT LINES

All companies everywhere have products and/or product lines that account for a heavy percentage of sales or profits. Many of these will be critical to the success of the company during the next year. It must also be recognized that some may be headed for serious trouble during the next year and cannot be counted on to contribute the same previous sales and profits. These must be replaced with up-and-coming new lines. Thus, strategically critical product lines include both new and old product lines.

Products and product lines should not always be considered as strategically critical simply because of their ability to contribute heavy sales and profits in the coming year. The Japanese have proven the wisdom of viewing products and markets with a long-run outlook. Automobiles could not have been considered as strategically critical to several Japanese manufacturers in the early years because of their short-run ability to contribute profits. Some products selected as strategically critical should be chosen for their probable value in assisting a company to meet its long-range goals. This is particularly important in international markets. Success in the international environment depends upon constancy of effort despite setbacks, discouragements, and lack of immediate profit.

"Strategic Planning" has come under attack. Many companies have responded by removing strategic planning from strictly a staff function to an operational level. Management will continue to struggle with this process for many years. Individuals who have responsibility for developing an operational marketing plan must give serious consideration to the concept of strategically critical product lines. In some cases, the solution will be dictated by top management. In others, operational marketing managers may have an opportunity to help select these products and work with top management to secure the resourses necessary to insure their long-run success.

PRODUCT LINE MARKETING STRATEGIES

Describe the marketing strategies for each product line that will be used during the next year to accomplish the previously stated objectives.

Product Line _____

Strategy _____

_____

_____

Product Line _____

Strategy _____

_____

_____

Product Line _____

Strategy _____

_____

_____

Product Line _____

Strategy _____

_____

_____

STRATEGICALLY CRITICAL PRODUCT LINE MARKETING STRATEGIES

Product Line _____

Strategy _____

_____

_____

Product Line _____

Strategy _____

_____

_____

Product Line _____

Strategy _____

_____

_____

Product Line _____

Strategy _____

_____

_____

19

Pricing

COMMENTARY

Prices for the next year must be established for each product line. The establishment of price is probably the most important decision within a marketing plan.

Prices are seldom, if ever, established by the marketing department. Marketing should have an input in discussions concerning pricing, but the final decision is generally established at higher levels of management.

Pricing objectives must match objectives for product lines. If they do not match, the marketing plan will be in conflict from the beginning. For example, if the corporate objective is to increase market share, it is questionable if a pricing objective of increasing price to offset last year's losses would be logical.

Some companies employ a pricing strategy of planning price reductions well in advance of competition by plotting production efficiencies along a learning curve. This forces competition to do likewise or seek small market niches.

Pricing strategies must be able to be verbalized and written. If pricing strategies cannot be expressed and defended, then pricing decisions probably reflect defensive "me too" moves or are based on a rule of thumb of X percent increase per year. These methods for making pricing decisions almost inevitably result in serious trouble for a firm.

PRODUCT LINE PRICING OBJECTIVES AND STRATEGIES 19____

Objectives — Sales Promotion

A. Describe the pricing objectives for each product line for 19____.

1. Product Line _____ Pricing Objective _____
   _____
   _____

2. Product Line _____ Pricing Objective _____
   _____
   _____

3. Product Line _____ Pricing Objective _____
   _____
   _____

Strategies — Promotion

B. Describe the pricing strategies for each product line for 19____.

1. Product Line _____ Pricing Strategy _____
   _____
   _____

2. Product Line _____ Pricing Strategy _____
   _____
   _____

3. Product Line _____ Pricing Strategy _____
   _____
   _____

PRICES AND PRICE CHANGES FOR PRODUCT LINES 19___

All Product Lines	Prices to End User	Dealer Prices	Prices to Distributors and Wholesalers	Percentage Price Change to End User compared to last year	Percent Price Change to Distributors compared to last year	Percentage Price Change to Dealer compared to last year
1.						
2.						
3.						
4.						
5.						
6.						
7.						
8.						
9.						
10.						

20

Channels of Distribution

COMMENTARY

The use of new channels of distribution frequently offers opportunities to gain a competitive edge. Warehouse club plans and direct mail are examples of new channels of distribution for many companies that have resulted in sales of hundreds of millions of dollars per year.

Other companies have discovered that older reliable channels such as door-to-door or party plan systems have shown dramatic declines in sales volume.

Electronic shopping and other new channels may produce large-volume sales for companies in the future. It is the responsibility of the marketing department to assess new channels of distribution, experiment with them, and then adopt them if the potential for reward seems higher than the risk.

Companies sometimes set distribution objectives such as gaining X percent of the established dealers in an area, or increasing the amount of shelf space in certain retail stores in a given area by X percent. Again, distribution objectives must match and support marketing objectives.

EXPERIMENTATION

The importance of achieving strong distribution has probably been understated in marketing literature. A company with strong distribution channels can sometimes successfully market a product that admittedly does not have the qualities of a stronger product with weak distribution.

Channels of distribution are not static. They often change dramatically within a decade or less. Companies must continuously experiment with new channels, and funds must be allocated for these experiments. If a company depends upon a salaried sales force, it is faced with a potentially serious problem. The cost of maintaining a salaried sales force can be astronomical. Imagine the potential problems facing such a company in the event of a serious gasoline shortage, a shortage of skilled salespeople, or the discovery and use of a less expensive distribution system by a major competitor.

Sometimes lucrative distribution systems are overlooked. Worldwide duty-free stores and military stores such as those operated by the U.S. Army-Air Force Exchange are examples of distribution channels that are sometimes overlooked.

A company in the furniture industry discovered that it could successfully sell furniture at state fairs, trade shows, and other events in which exhibitors could rent space. Other furniture companies sell their products on vacant lots, in tents, or off-the-truck. These are not traditional outlets and are not good outlets for all competitors, but they present market niche opportunities for some.

An Australian company uses special vending machines in rest rooms to sell a plastic tube that contains a disposable toothbrush complete with toothpaste. Burger King has experimented with a mobile restaurant and a large Mexican food manufacturer has established a branded Mexican food section at a south-eastern university. Normally, the brand names of processed foods are lost in restaurants and cafeterias. The experiment in a university cafeteria allowed the manufacturer to display its brand name at the point-of-purchase for the students in the cafeteria.

Distribution experiments do not always require dramatic changes in terms of finding new channels. Hartz Mountain was able to acquire end-of-aisle display space in supermarkets, where it had previously sold its products on the shelves.

Consumer products companies have discovered that they can enter institutional markets with packaging modifications. Several cosmetic companies sell their products to upscale hotels for free distribution to guests in their rooms. This new distribution channel increases sales and provides greater consumer exposure to the products and brands of a company.

Ideas for new channels of distribution come from many sources. Keeping one's eyes, ears, and mind open to opportunities, and then being willing to experiment, are the keys to success in gaining new channels of distribution.

DISTRIBUTION OBJECTIVES AND STRATEGIES 19____

Distribution Objectives 19____

Describe the distribution objectives for next year.

Product Line _____ Distribution Objectives _____

_____

Product Line _____ Distribution Objectives _____

_____

Product Line _____ Distribution Objectives _____

_____

Distribution Strategies 19____

Describe next year's distribution strategies for each product line.

Product Line _____ Distribution Strategies _____

_____

Product Line _____ Distribution Strategies _____

_____

Product Line _____ Distribution Strategies _____

_____

Describe changes in distribution strategies compared to last year.

DESCRIPTION OF CHANNELS OF DISTRIBUTION NEEDED FOR 19_____

Channels of Distribution	Sales Volume Number	Units	Dollars	Percent of Total Sales	Average Monthly Sales Vol. per Each
Company-Owned Retail Outlets					
Independent Retail Outlets					
Sales Force — Salaried					
Sales Force — Commissioned					
Wholesalers/Distributors Company-Owned					
Wholesalers/Distributors Independent					
Other Outlets					

DESCRIPTION OF CHANNELS OF DISTRIBUTION NEEDED FOR 19____

Retail Outlets

Company-Owned Stores (by name)	Sales Units	Volume Dollars	Percent of Total Sales	Ranking by Sales	Average Monthly Sales Volume
_____					
_____					
_____					
_____					
_____					
_____					
_____					
_____					
_____					
_____					
_____					
_____					
_____					
_____					
Independent Retail Outlets (by name)					
_____					
_____					
_____					
_____					
_____					
_____					
_____					
_____					

DESCRIPTION OF CHANNELS OF DISTRIBUTION NEEDED FOR 19____

Wholesalers/Distributors (by name)	Sales Volume Units	Dollars	Percent of Total Sales	Ranking by Sales	Average Monthly Sales Volume
_____					
_____					
_____					
_____					
_____					
_____					
_____					
_____					
_____					
_____					
_____					
Other Distribution Outlets (by name)					
_____					
_____					
_____					
_____					
_____					
_____					
_____					
_____					
_____					

21

Marketing Personnel

COMMENTARY

One of the most difficult tasks facing any manager is to inform an employee that he or she is no longer needed. It is always easier and more pleasant to add rather than reduce staff. In the absence of serious personnel planning, a company will often be under- or overstaffed.

This section calls for the marketing planner to determine more than dollar expenditures for next year's personnel. It forces the manager to determine the percentage of sales vs. nonsales personnel and to determine personnel costs as a percentage of sales revenue.

Marketing departments sometimes become overstaffed with nonsales people. Remember that nothing in the company can happen unless sales are made. Strategic planning, marketing research, and other support functions are useful, but they sometimes gain in numbers at the expense of additions to the sales force.

There is no room in any company for nonproductive salespeople. These forms will force a manager to make assessments about the future sales of all members of the sales force. If the numbers look bleak for certain members, corrective measures will have to be taken, including replacement.

COMMENTARY—PERSONAL SALES QUOTAS AND OBJECTIVES

Company sales objectives are seldom met by accident. They are achieved through conscious and continuous planning and control.

Follow-through in the field is essential to insure that the cumulative sales of all members of the sales force equate with monthly and annual corporate sales objectives.

Quotas

Each member of the sales force, regardless of tenure, must have a sales quota by month and by year. In some companies, the monthly quota is determined solely by the sales manager/s. In others, the salesperson is assigned annual, and/or semiannual and/or quarterly quotas. Sales quotas represent a minimum level of sales expected by the company. *They do not represent maximum sales.*

Sales quotas are often unequal for members of the sales force. It is common for members to have lower quotas than more experienced salespeople. It is also common for quotas to reflect the market potential of a territory. Since territories with equal market potential are generally impossible to establish, it is common for sales managers to assign higher quotas to territories with greater potential.

Companies sometimes use open territories in which no salesperson has a protected area. In this case, it is common to find that all established members of the sales force have a similar quota.

Different quotas are often established by product line. If quotas are not set by product line, it is common for members of the sales force to concentrate on products that are the easiest to sell. Products with the highest profit margin and new products often suffer. Quotas may be set to insure that the entire product line is sold. In these cases, hard-to-sell product lines usually have a lower quota.

Short-Term Quotas

It is difficult for most people to think and plan in terms of annual sales objectives. Successful salespeople have discovered that they must plan objectives for shorter periods of time. Monthly, weekly, and daily objectives help in planning.

If sales quotas and objectives are reviewed weekly, there is time for the salesperson and the sales manager to analyze the problem and take corrective action. If sales quotas and objectives are reviewed only quarterly or annually, there is little or no opportunity for corrective action. This leads to discontent on the part of both the salesperson and management.

Continued negative deviation from quota is a serious matter that will demand action by a sales manager. Continued sales well above quota serve as a self-motivating device. When a salesperson marks another month of sales that meet or exceed personal objectives, personal enthusiasm and self-respect are high. Pride in one's accomplishments is the greatest motivator of all.

Personal Objectives

Companies with exceptional sales records expect exceptional results from the sales force. Exceptional sales are the result of highly motivated and talented salespeople who are not content with merely meeting quotas.

Exceptional sales are seldom achieved by simply increasing quotas. This can have a negative psychological impact upon the sales force. Instead, members of the sales force are encouraged to establish personal sales objectives above quotas. It is the responsibility of management to help members of the sales force to realize these objectives. Educational programs, sales contests, motivational messages, peer recognition, and other tactics are used to help salespeople accomplish objectives well above quota.

Use of These Forms

These forms allow a salesperson to see clearly what is expected in terms of sales by unit and by dollar. Some companies record sales only by units or dollars and the unnecessary column may be eliminated.

Sales by product line is a very common measure of sales performance. However, some companies use other measures such as sales by territory. Use only the information most relevant to your company.

MARKETING PERSONNEL NEEDED BY REGION

Next Year's Marketing Personnel Budget $_____
Next Year's Marketing Personnel Headcount_____

	Numbers Total Current Year	Region 1	Region 2	Region 3
Salaried				
Managerial (List)				
(1)				
(2)				
(3)				
(4)				
Sales Force Salaried				
(1)				
(2)				
(3)				
(4)				
Sales Force Commission				
(1)				
(2)				
(3)				
(4)				
Office — Clerical				
Secretarial				
(1)				
(2)				
(3)				
(4)				
Other				
(1)				
(2)				
(3)				
(4)				
Total Personnel				

MARKETING PERSONNEL NUMBERS AND EXPENDITURES BY MONTH FOR 19____

	Jan Units	$'s	Feb Units	$'s	Mar Units	$'s	Apr Units	$'s	May Units	$'s	Jun Units	$'s
Salaried Managerial (List)												
(1)												
(2)												
(3)												
(4)												
Sales Force Salaried												
(1)												
(2)												
(3)												
(4)												
Sales Force Commission												
(1)												
(2)												
(3)												
(4)												
Office – Clerical Secretarial												
(1)												
(2)												
(3)												
(4)												
Other												
(1)												
(2)												
(3)												
(4)												
Total Personnel												

MARKETING PERSONNEL NUMBERS AND EXPENDITURES BY MONTH FOR 19____

	Jul Units	$'s	Aug Units	$'s	Sep Units	$'s	Oct Units	$'s	Nov Units	$'s	Dec Units	$'s
Salaried Managerial (List)												
(1)												
(2)												
(3)												
(4)												
Sales Force Salaried												
(1)												
(2)												
(3)												
(4)												
Sales Force Commission												
(1)												
(2)												
(3)												
(4)												
Office — Clerical Secretarial												
(1)												
(2)												
(3)												
(4)												
Other												
(1)												
(2)												
(3)												
(4)												
Total Personnel												

SALES FORCE NEEDED FOR 19____

Sales Force	Sales Units	Volume Dollars	Percent of Total Sales	Ranking by Sales	Average Monthly Sales Volume
Sales Force Members (by name)					
_____					
_____					
_____					
_____					
_____					
_____					
_____					
_____					
_____					
_____					
_____					
_____					
_____					
_____					
_____					
_____					
_____					
_____					

SALES FORCE NEEDED FOR 19____

Sales Force	Years Experience	Education	Salary	Commission Bonus	Expense
Sales Force Members (by name)					
_____					
_____					
_____					
_____					
_____					
_____					
_____					
_____					
_____					
_____					
_____					
_____					
_____					
_____					
_____					
_____					
_____					
_____					
_____					
_____					
_____					
_____					

NEXT YEAR'S MARKETING PERSONNEL EXPENDITURES INFORMATION 19____

Number in Sales Force _____

Number Non-Sales Personnel _____

Total Number in Marketing Dept. _____

Dollar Expenditures for Sales Force (direct costs) $_____

Dollar Expenditures for Non-Sales Personnel $_____

Total Expenditures for Marketing Personnel $_____

Percent of Total Marketing Budget – Sales Force _____%

Percent of Total Marketing Budget-Non-Sales Personnel _____%

Sales Force Expenditures as Percent of Sales _____%

Non-Sales Personnel Expenditures as Percent of Sales _____%

22

Human Resource Development

COMMENTARY

If a company is going to achieve its objectives, it must have employees who are trained and motivated. An investment in training for members of the marketing department often results in excellent long-run gains.

Today, many colleges and universities no longer teach courses in salesmanship. The basics of sales and sales management can often be acquired only through private programs. Conferences and seminars offer opportunities for members of the marketing department to develop their skills in marketing research, strategic planning, advertising, and many other areas.

Employees respond to opportunities to learn by exhibiting a more positive attitude toward their workplace and their employer.

It is critical to determine what skills need sharpening. Marketing departments aren't high schools or colleges and can't assume the duties of these institutions. They should be expected to offer employees the opportunity to continue to learn concepts and skills that will directly benefit them on the job.

It will benefit management to keep abreast of training opportunities for employees. Many managers maintain files of programs offered by private companies, associations, and universities, and select those that best fit their needs.

In-house training programs offered by members of the company, including marketing managers, are especially valuable. The objectives and costs associated with these and all training programs should be carefully considered and entered into the marketing plan.

SOURCES OF EDUCATIONAL—TRAINING PROGRAMS

Education—Training Needs

Need	Possible Sources of Assistance
Technical Skills and Interpersonal Skills	In-House Programs Technical Institutes, Colleges, Universities Private Consultants; Instructors Professional Associations

Technical skill training needed for marketing employees is relatively inexpensive and easy to locate, unlike training needs in other departments such as manufacturing or pilot training. Secretarial/clerical skills and use of a personal computer are among the most common skill training needs for marketing. These can be obtained through established programs in midsized and larger cities.

Other needs might include marketing research or advertising skills. These are generally confined to updating material or learning new techniques, which can be accomplished through seminars.

Interpersonal skills are commonly sharpened through programs such as Dale Carnegie or those offered at local colleges or universities. Occasionally, nonprofit community groups such as the Chamber of Commerce will sponsor this type of course. Organizations have also made use of programs such as Outward Bound. A large North Carolina bank has a contract with a large fire department to provide a program that demands learning new skills such as rappelling. There is mixed opinion concerning the usefulness of programs that have a "survival" or "wilderness" orientation in terms of application to a marketing department.

Retired employees and outside consultants often provide custom-designed programs to sharpen interpersonal skills. It is important to check credentials carefully prior to hiring outside consultants. It is also critical to thoroughly understand and agree with the objectives and learning methodology to be employed.

There are organizations and individuals who use highly questionable methods to obtain objectives which are also sometimes questionable. A marketing department has sufficient problems without adding more as a result of "trendy" or "flaky" interpersonal training programs.

	Examples
Product Knowledge	In-House Programs
	Vendors; Suppliers
	Trade Shows

Product information is best transmitted through in-house personnel and representatives from suppliers. Travel agencies frequently ask representatives from airlines, cruise ships, auto rental agencies, and others to meet with the sales staff and conduct short seminars concerning their company's travel-related services.

Attendance at trade shows can also serve as a useful conduit for product knowledge. Most companies restrict attendance at trade shows since these are costly and can be counterproductive if used primarily as the excuse for a party.

The single best source of product knowledge available to a marketing department consists of managers and knowledgeable staff within other departments. There is a benefit to be gained by exposing marketing personnel to other departments, having them spend a few days in each. This requires the close cooperation of other department heads. In some industries this involves physical risks. A large bakery used to require all white collar employees to work for a few days at the ovens until a trainee fainted from exhaustion and heat exposure. It is also important to recognize that on-the-job programs sometimes create conflicts with the union if nonunionized employees are placed in union positions for even short periods of time.

	Examples
Organization Knowledge	In-House Programs

In-house training programs represent the single best source of information about the organization. Training aids such as professional videotapes may be used but these require guidance from an experienced company employee.

Informal training programs often work best within the marketing department. A Friday afternoon session in which managers and staff from other departments share comments with the marketing department can be highly productive.

	Examples
Market-Environment Knowledge	In-House Programs
	Colleges, Universities
	Private Consultants
	Professional Associations

Marketing managers want specific information about specific markets. This is best accomplished by using private consultants or in-house staff to develop seminars or updates about markets.

Occasionally, marketers are interested in learning about general changes which may affect markets. International updates including political analyses of regions are sometimes offered by associations or colleges and universities. Authors such as Alvin Toffler have written about trends that affect a nation. This information is often of interest to marketers and is sometimes available through public seminars conducted by the author.

	Examples
Managerial Improvement	Colleges and Universities
	Associations
	Public Seminars

Managerial improvement programs are numerous. They range from one-day seminars to programs lasting several weeks. The quality of these programs is highly varied. Prior to selecting any, it is wise to check with individuals who have taken the program. Prices also vary greatly. A price of $500 per day per participant is not unusual for seminars.

	Examples
Self-Motivation and Personal Problems	Associations
	Public Seminars
	Self-Help Groups
	Religious Groups

Caution! Examine these programs with extreme care before using them. Remember, anyone can offer a seminar regardless of experience or training. There are valuable programs of this type, but check out references before enrolling employees.

	Examples
General Knowledge	Colleges and Universities
	Museums, Historic Restorations, Art Galleries, and Other Public Institutions

This is an area in which colleges and universities excel. There are also excellent programs available through museums, nature-science centers, zoos, and other public institutions. There is an abundance of high-quality programs. Marketing managers must decide if the expenditure is worthwhile. Does it really pay to encourage and support marketing personnel to pursue general knowledge programs that have little or no direct relevancy to the company?

HUMAN RESOURCE DEVELOPMENT OBJECTIVES AND STRATEGIES FOR 19_____

Objectives — Human Resource Development

A. Describe next year's Human Resource Development Objectives.

   1. Human Resource Development Objective _____

     _____

     _____

   2. Human Resource Development Objective _____

     _____

     _____

   3. Human Resource Development Objective _____

     _____

     _____

Strategies — Human Resource Development

B. Describe next year's Human Resource Development Strategies.

   1. Human Resource Development Strategy _____

     _____

     _____

   2. Human Resource Development Strategy _____

     _____

     _____

   3. Human Resource Development Strategy _____

     _____

     _____

19_____ HUMAN RESOURCE DEVELOPMENT BUDGET $_____

Human Resource Development Program

	Next Year's Expenditures	Describe
Sales Training		
Programs		
Aids		
Other		
Executive Development		
Programs		
Aids		
Other		
Nonsales Development		
Programs		
Aids		
Other		
Other		

HUMAN RESOURCE DEVELOPMENT EXPENDITURES INFORMATION

1. Human resource development expenditures as a percent of total sales.   _____%

2. Human resource development expenditures as a percent of total marketing budget.   _____%

3. Human resource development expenditures vs. industry average.   _____%

23

Marketing Research Program

COMMENTARY

Marketing research does not need to be expensive. It is true that many studies can cost $100,000 or more, but not all companies require that level of research.

It is often possible to obtain marketing research work through graduate schools in which MBA students conduct research as part of their training. Marketing research firms provide studies at a variety of costs. The key is knowing what is needed and shopping for value.

Marketing research cannot offer all the answers to marketing problems. For example, it can seldom really answer the question of why consumers do what they do. Marketing research is of real value in determining trends; providing an estimate of market potential; providing demographic and psychographic descriptions of customers and noncustomers; providing information about competitors; providing information about new markets; and providing clues to the way consumers feel about products.

Marketing research will never be a substitute for knowledge and experience, but can greatly assist even the most experienced executive to make better decisions.

It definitely has a role in industrial, consumer, and service firms, and a budget allocation should be made for marketing research. If marketing research has not been used in your firm, it might be wise to ask the opinions of specialists in the field, such as marketing research firms, how they can assist in the marketing management process within your company. Often there is no charge for this advice from those who sell marketing research services. Don't be afraid to ask more than one firm. A second opinion never hurts.

KEEPING ABREAST OF NEW TECHNOLOGY AND TECHNIQUES

The field of marketing research has undergone substantial change. New techniques and technology appear continuously. Some are quite sophisticated; others are improvements of traditional techniques.

A variety of professional seminars are offered by universities, private companies, and associations.

The American Marketing Association offers a variety of conferences and seminars, and also publishes a journal in the field of marketing research. This organization also offers a variety of professional programs in the entire field of marketing. You should consider membership in this organization, if you or your company are not currently enrolled. Write or phone:

American Marketing Association
Suite 200
250 S. Wacker Drive
Chicago, Illinois 60606-5819
(312) 648-0536

MARKETING RESEARCH OBJECTIVES AND STRATEGIES FOR 19____

Objectives: Describe next year's marketing research objectives for each product line.

Product Line _____ Marketing Research Objective _____

_____

Product Line _____ Marketing Research Objective _____

_____

Product Line _____ Marketing Research Objective _____

_____

Strategies: Describe next year's marketing research strategies for each product line.

Product Line _____ Marketing Research Strategies _____

_____

Product Line _____ Marketing Research Strategies _____

_____

Product Line _____ Marketing Research Strategies _____

_____

19____ MARKETING RESEARCH BUDGET $____

Marketing Research Projects

Product Research	Expenditures	Describe
(1) Current Line		
(2) New Products		
Advertising Research		
Corporate Research (Image, Logo, etc.)		
Other Research		
_____		
_____		
_____		
_____		

MARKETING RESEARCH EXPENDITURES INFORMATION 19____

1. Marketing expenditures as a percent of total sales.   _____%

2. Marketing research expenditures as a percent of total marketing budget.   _____%

3. Marketing research expenditures vs. industry average.   _____%

24

Advertising and Sales Promotion Program

COMMENTARY

Advertising

Prior to allocating an advertising budget, it is essential to determine what is desired of advertising. Many people are impressed by seeing their company's name and products in an advertisement, but does this help sell the product? Advertising is an effective tool. It is also expensive and can be wasteful.

Determine what it is you want advertising to accomplish, and then how you might evaluate the effectiveness of your advertising. Don't be led down an ever-increasing blind alley of higher advertising costs. Ask yourself this: Am I really getting my money's worth or should I spend this money on additional salespeople, training, or another form of promotion?

Sales Promotion

There is disagreement as to what sales promotion means. Some companies use the term to include couponing, public relations, and specialty advertising. It doesn't really matter. The end result has to be increased sales, greater market share, or the accomplishment of some other measurable objective. Sales promotion must accomplish what the term implies. It must promote sales. If it doesn't, a company is supporting gamesmanship. Determine in advance how sales promotion results will be measured. Don't buy the line that this is impossible. Remember that the objective is to support sales.

Advertising Effectiveness

What is meant by advertising effectiveness? There is no single answer applicable to all companies. The effectiveness of advertising must be judged against the stated objectives. Examples of advertising effectiveness include:

Sales Increase — The effect of advertising upon sales is usually very difficult to measure. Many factors, in addition to advertising, may influence sales. Direct mail, or advertisements within media that require a direct response from the consumer, such as placing an order through an 800 number, are examples of cases in which the effectiveness of advertisements can be measured. Nevertheless, the purpose of most advertising is to increase sales, and it is important for the company and the advertising agency to give serious thought to this need and to continuously attempt to measure this important link between advertising and sales.

Advances in marketing research now permit professionals in the field to test advertisements among targeted consumers in test markets, and to measure their purchase patterns at local retail outlets.

Reader-Listener-Viewer Response Rate — How many consumers mailed or sent a reply by mail in response to advertising? Reader cards inserted in trade magazines serve this purpose.

Recall — How many readers, viewers, or listeners were able to recall a particular advertisement? How many recalled seeing or hearing the name of a product or company?

Recall and Association — How many readers, viewers, or listeners not only recalled seeing a particular advertisement, but also correctly identified it with the right brand?

Physiological — There are individuals and organizations who claim to measure advertising effectiveness through a variety of physiological responses such as eye blinks or gaze patterns.

Advertising and Sales Promotion Expenditure Ratios — Marketing professionals are often asked, "What percentage of sales or what percentage of costs should I allocate to advertising and sales promotion?" A simple answer such as X percent of sales should not be given; yet management often continues to demand these measures. The only acceptable answer should be based on expenditures that are sufficient to accomplish objectives including a desired profit level.

Many industries have historically used ratios and percentages to budget advertising and sales promotion expenditures such as X dollars per barrel of beer or ton of product produced or dozens of cartons.

There are many examples in which management decided to abandon these rules of thumb and spend disproportionately more than anyone in the entire industry. The result has sometimes been a dramatic increase in sales and market share.

Since ratios and percentages are commonly demanded by management, it is well to include them in a marketing plan. *Warning:* Be prepared to defend expenditures that are higher than industry averages or are higher than historical expenditure patterns for the company. If industry expenditure patterns are above those for your company, this evidence may be used to obtain higher budget allocations. Having once used ratios or percentages as a tool, management may expect you to continue, and may judge future budget requests against these norms rather than against objectives.

ADVERTISING OBJECTIVES AND STRATEGIES FOR 19____

A. Describe next year's advertising objectives for each existing product line.

1. Product Line _____ Advertising Objectives _____

_____

_____

2. Product Line _____ Advertising Objectives _____

_____

_____

3. Product Line _____ Advertising Objectives _____

_____

_____

4. Product Line _____ Advertising Objectives _____

_____

_____

B. Describe next year's advertising strategies for each existing product line.

1. Product Line _____ Advertising Strategies _____

_____

_____

2. Product Line _____ Advertising Strategies _____

_____

_____

3. Product Line _____ Advertising Strategies _____

_____

_____

4. Product Line _____ Advertising Strategies _____

_____

_____

C. Describe the advertising objectives for each new product line to be introduced next year. 19___

   1. New Product _____ Advertising Objectives _____

_____

_____

   2. New Product _____ Advertising Objectives _____

_____

_____

   3. New Product _____ Advertising Objectives _____

_____

_____

   4. New Product _____ Advertising Objectives _____

_____

_____

D. Describe the advertising strategies for each new product line to be introduced next year. 19___

   1. New Product _____ Advertising Strategies _____

_____

_____

   2. New Product _____ Advertising Strategies _____

_____

_____

   3. New Product _____ Advertising Strategies _____

_____

_____

   4. New Product _____ Advertising Strategies _____

_____

_____

19____ ADVERTISING MEDIA PROGRAM AND BUDGET

Advertising Budget $ ____

Media	Annual $ Expenditures	Frequency	Ad Size
Print			
Newspaper			
(1)_____			
(2)_____			
(3)_____			
Consumer Magazine			
(1)_____			
(2)_____			
(3)_____			
Trade Publication			
(1)_____			
(2)_____			
(3)_____			
Radio			
AM (1)_____			
(2)_____			
(3)_____			
FM (1)_____			
(2)_____			
(3)_____			
Television			
(1)_____			
(2)_____			
(3)_____			
Specialty			
(1)_____			
(2)_____			
(3)_____			
Direct Mail			
(1)_____			
(2)_____			
(3)_____			
Point of Purchase			
(1)_____			
(2)_____			
(3)_____			
Co-op			
(1)_____			
(2)_____			
(3)_____			
Other			
(1)_____			
(2)_____			
(3)_____			

ADVERTISING EXPENDITURES BY MONTH
BY MEDIA FOR 19____

Media	Jan $'s	Feb $'s	Mar $'s	Apr $'s	May $'s	Jun $'s
Print						
Newspaper						
(1)_____						
(2)_____						
(3)_____						
Consumer Magazine						
(1)_____						
(2)_____						
(3)_____						
Trade Publication						
(1)_____						
(2)_____						
(3)_____						
Radio						
AM (1)_____						
(2)_____						
(3)_____						
FM (1)_____						
(2)_____						
(3)_____						
Television						
(1)_____						
(2)_____						
(3)_____						
Specialty						
(1)_____						
(2)_____						
(3)_____						
Direct Mail						
(1)_____						
(2)_____						
(3)_____						
Point of Purchase						
(1)_____						
(2)_____						
(3)_____						
Co-op						
(1)_____						
(2)_____						
(3)_____						
Other						
(1)_____						
(2)_____						
(3)_____						

ADVERTISING EXPENDITURES BY MONTH
BY MEDIA FOR 19____

Media	Jul $'s	Aug $'s	Sep $'s	Oct $'s	Nov $'s	Dec $'s
Print						
Newspaper						
(1)_____						
(2)_____						
(3)_____						
Consumer Magazine						
(1)_____						
(2)_____						
(3)_____						
Trade Publication						
(1)_____						
(2)_____						
(3)_____						
Radio						
AM (1)_____						
(2)_____						
(3)_____						
FM (1)_____						
(2)_____						
(3)_____						
Television						
(1)_____						
(2)_____						
(3)_____						
Specialty						
(1)_____						
(2)_____						
(3)_____						
Direct Mail						
(1)_____						
(2)_____						
(3)_____						
Point of Purchase						
(1)_____						
(2)_____						
(3)_____						
Co-op						
(1)_____						
(2)_____						
(3)_____						
Other						
(1)_____						
(2)_____						
(3)_____						

ADVERTISING AGENCY INFORMATION FOR 19____

Agency/ies to be used

Product lines for which advertising agency has responsibility

In-House Agency _____   _____

Outside Agency _____   _____

Address   _____

Phone Number   _____

Telex or Cable   _____

Account Executive   _____

Describe Responsibility of Advertising Agency _____

_____

Compensation System for Advertising Agency _____

_____

191

ADVERTISING EFFECTIVENESS

List and describe methods to be used to measure effectiveness of advertising for 19___.

Products   *Method to Measure Effectiveness*

Strategically Critical Product Lines

New Products

Product Line in General

Person/s Responsible for Measuring Advertising Effectiveness

ADVERTISING EXPENDITURES INFORMATION 19____

1. Advertising Expenditures As a Percent of Total Sales. _____%

2. Advertising Expenditures As a Percent of Total Marketing Budget. _____%

3. Advertising Expenditures vs. Industry Average. _____%

SALES PROMOTION OBJECTIVES AND STRATEGIES FOR 19____

Objectives — Sales Promotion

A. Describe next year's promotion objectives for each existing product line.

1. Product Line _____ Sales Promotion Objective _____

_____

_____

2. Product Line _____ Sales Promotion Objective _____

_____

_____

3. Product Line _____ Sales Promotion Objective _____

_____

_____

Strategies — Sales Promotion

B. Describe next year's Sales Promotion Strategies for each existing product line.

1. Product Line _____ Sales Promotion Strategies _____

_____

_____

2. Product Line _____ Sales Promotion Strategies _____

_____

_____

3. Product Line _____ Sales Promotion Strategies _____

_____

_____

NEXT YEAR'S SALES PROMOTION OBJECTIVES AND STRATEGIES

Describe next year's sales promotion objectives and strategies for each new product line to be introduced.

1. New Product Line_____

   Sales Promotion Objectives_____

   Sales Promotion Strategy_____

2. New Product Line_____

   Sales Promotion Objectives_____

   Sales Promotion Strategy_____

3. New Product Line_____

   Sales Promotion Objectives_____

   Sales Promotion Strategy_____

4. New Product Line_____

   Sales Promotion Objectives_____

   Sales Promotion Strategy_____

SALES PROMOTION EXPENDITURES BY ITEM BY MONTH FOR 19____

Sales Promotion Budget $____

Types of Sales
Promotion

	Jan $'s		Feb $'s		Mar $'s		Apr $'s		May $'s		Jun $'s
Trade Promos to Dealers and Distributors											
Trade Shows											
Sales Force Promotion											
Other Sales Promotion											
Totals (Must Equal Sales Promotion Budget)											

SALES PROMOTION EXPENDITURES BY ITEM BY MONTH FOR 19____

Sales Promotion Budget $____

Types of Sales
Promotion

	Jul $'s	Aug $'s	Sep $'s	Oct $'s	Nov $'s	Dec $'s	Year $ Total	% of SP Budget
Trade Promos to Dealers and Distributors								
Trade Shows								
Sales Force Promotion								
Other Sales Promotion								
Totals (Must Equal Sales Promotion Budget)								

SALES PROMOTION AGENCY INFORMATION FOR 19_____

Agency/ies to be used.

Product lines for which advertising agency has responsibility

In-House Agency_____   _____

Outside Agency_____   _____

Address   _____

Phone Number   _____

Telex or Cable   _____

Account Executive   _____

Describe Responsibility of Sales Promotion Agency_____

_____

_____

Compensation System for Sales Promotion Agency_____

_____

_____

SALES PROMOTION EFFECTIVENESS

List and describe methods to be used to measure effectiveness of sales promotion.

Sales Promotion Activity   *Method to Measure Effectiveness*

1.

2.

3.

4.

5.

6.

Person/s responsible for measuring sales promotion effectiveness.

SALES PROMOTION EXPENDITURES INFORMATION

1. Sales promotion expenditures as percent of total sales.   _____%

2. Sales promotion expenditures as percent of total marketing budget.   _____%

3. Sales promotion expenditures vs. industry average   _____%

25

Marketing Budget

COMMENTARY

A well-prepared marketing budget can be used as an effective tool by those responsible for marketing activities to obtain needed budget allocations from top management. If a marketing budget is not prepared and defended by marketing, this department will normally be given a figure by management and told to live within the constraints. This amount may not be sufficient to accomplish the preferred marketing strategies to meet objectives.

It is the responsibility of the marketing department to carefully prepare a proposed budget which reflects projected costs associated with the proposed marketing plan. This budget should then be presented and defended in the presence of higher management.

Many companies still base next year's marketing budget on some rules of thumb such as (a) a percentage gain over last year's budget, or (b) a percentage of sales such as X percent per ton of product sold last year. This system of budget allocation is not in tune with the concept of developing and using a marketing plan to meet objectives which were determined through a careful examination of the market.

Unless marketing managers are willing to build and defend marketing budgets, their departments will continue to depend on allocations derived from formulas and rules of thumb which seldom reflect existing market conditions and opportunities.

An example of a simple marketing budget form has been included in this section. Several expenditure items would need to be deleted or added to match the needs of a marketing department. It is also possible that a marketing manager will want to use a budget that reflects monthly budget forecasts rather than quarterly budget forecasts.

The placement of items within the budget will depend on company policy and procedures, tradition, and other factors.

The placement of individual items within the budget is relatively unimportant as long as all expenditure items are included. Sometimes, items placed in one area are more likely to receive favorable attention by management than others. For instance, the president may believe strongly in personal sales and have little confidence in the role of advertising. In this situation, a marketing manager would undoubtedly decide to allocate more expenses under sales than under marketing. Items such as secretarial assistance may appear in several areas of the marketing budget based on cost allocation to marketing areas, or these costs may be grouped under one heading such as General and Administrative. A marketing manager is well advised to seek assistance from the accounting department and others in the company before preparing forms for a marketing budget.

All companies have their own systems for developing a budget. The sample shown in this section was not designed to reflect the "best" way to prepare a budget, nor was it intended to reflect the order or completeness of items to be included.

The development of a marketing budget is generally viewed as one of the least desirable responsibilities by marketing and sales managers. The task should be shared with others in the marketing area and with professionals such as advertising agencies. This includes managers who are responsible for: (a) secretarial, clerical, and office supplies; (b) advertising and sales promotion; (c) marketing research; (d) sales; (e) others.

Middle-level managers within the marketing department should be expected to provide estimates of the needs facing their areas of responsibility for the coming year. Realistic estimates of resource and monetary support are dependent upon an understanding of objectives for the next year.

Unfortunately, many organizations expect those developing budget estimates to accomplish this task without knowing where the company is headed next year, or what it expects to accomplish. The process of establishing budgets and the process of establishing objectives cannot be separated. If one is done without knowledge of the other, the company will be in harmony during the next year purely by accident.

MARKETING BUDGET BY QUARTERS

Marketing Expenditures	Quarter I		Quarter II		Quarter III		Quarter IV	
	$	Percent Marketing Budget	$	Percent Marketing Budget	$	Percent Marketing Budget	$	Percent Marketing Budget
Advertising								
Newspaper								
Consumer Magazine								
Trade Publication								
Radio AM								
Radio FM								
Television								
Specialty								
Direct Mail								
Point of Purchase								
Co-op								
Other								
Sales Promotion								
Trade Promos – Dealers								
Trade Shows								
Sales Force Promotion								
Other Sales Promotions								
General and Administrative								
Clerical								
Managerial								
Secretarial								
Telephone								

MARKETING BUDGET BY QUARTERS

General and Administrative, continued	Quarter I		Quarter II		Quarter III		Quarter IV	
	$	Percent Marketing Budget	$	Percent Marketing Budget	$	Percent Marketing Budget	$	Percent Marketing Budget
Travel								
Supplies								
_____								
_____								
_____								
Human Resource Development								
Filmstrips								
In-house Program								
Tuition Rebate								
_____								
_____								
_____								
Sales Force Expenditures								
Motivation Program								
Recruiting								
Salaries and Benefits								
Telephone								
Training Program								
Travel								
_____								
_____								
_____								

MARKETING BUDGET BY QUARTERS

Marketing Research	Quarter I $	Percent Marketing Budget	Quarter II $	Percent Marketing Budget	Quarter III $	Percent Marketing Budget	Quarter IV $	Percent Marketing Budget
Computer Time								
Salaries and Benefits								
Supplies								
Telephone								
Travel								
_____								
_____								
_____								
Miscellaneous								
_____								
_____								
_____								

26

Marketing Activities Timetable

COMMENTARY

A primary responsibility of marketing managers is to determine and prioritize essential marketing activities. These are the activities which support marketing strategies and are sometimes referred to as tactics.

The complexity of this task depends on the size of the company, number of product lines, and available support staff. In a small company, one person may have responsibility for planning and implementing all marketing activities including sales force management, advertising, marketing research, and others. In larger companies, department managers will be responsible for the planning and supervision of activities.

Regardless, marketing activity or action calendars are helpful to insure that the key activities are completed as scheduled. It is otherwise all too easy to forget or postpone vital activities which can seriously interrupt or destroy the best designed marketing strategy.

Many types of action calendars are used by managers, ranging from a single desk calendar to techniques such as a PERT chart. A sample of an easy-to-follow action plan is included in this section. This action plan calls for a manager to identify the action step and to identify by initials or name the person to whom responsibility for completion of this task was assigned. The open triangle represents the month in which the activity is due to be completed. Once the activity has been completed, the triangle should be filled in to indicate completion.

Periodic progress reviews should be held and all managers should be required to indicate their progress in completing tasks. The time interval between periodic reviews varies widely between companies. In general these reviews should be held at least monthly. Many companies hold weekly reviews. The marketing activity timetable can easily be converted into a transparency and used on an overhead projector during regular meetings.

It is human nature to cover up problems in the completion of activities. The reason for regularly scheduled review meetings is to uncover problems and take corrective action before they become major impediments to the success of the marketing department.

MARKETING ACTIVITIES TIMETABLE

DEPT. _____

DEPT. MGR. _____

PRODUCT LINE _____

KEY: ▲ COMPLETED   △ NOT COMPLETED BUT DUE

ACTION STEPS	ASSIGNED	JAN	FEB	MAR	APR	MAY	JUN	JUL	AUG	SEP	OCT	NOV	DEC

27

Reviews and Evaluations

COMMENTARY

The effectiveness of a marketing plan must be objectively evaluated by management during scheduled periods. The marketing activity timetable serves as a means to insure that critical action events are accomplished on time. However, reviews are also needed to objectively appraise the effectiveness of the plan.

A perfect marketing plan does not exist. In spite of the best planning, situations can change which force marketing objectives and strategies to be altered or entirely scrapped. Outside variables beyond the control of marketing managers, such as economic conditions, changes in laws, devastating natural phenomena such as earthquakes or floods, and unexpected changes in competitive strategies, can create the need to modify marketing plans.

Normally, management will not be faced with the need to rapidly and dramatically change marketing plans. Consequently, it is easy to be lured into complacency.

The use of regularly scheduled evaluations provides an opportunity to make slight corrections if needed to insure that year-end objectives will be met. Major problems can normally be prevented before they occur. The situation is analogous to conducting regular maintenance on a vehicle rather than waiting for a breakdown which requires substantial time and money to repair.

The forms in this workbook call for monthly, quarterly, and year-end reviews. With the assistance of computers, more frequent reviews are possible. Many companies employ weekly reviews. It is suggested that at a minimum, monthly reviews become an established part of the responsibility of marketing management.

The form shown here requires a review of the sales in dollars and units for all product lines and has been designed for use by the head of the marketing department. The performance of each member of the sales force, each geographical area, and each subdivision of the department must also be regularly evaluated by the managers responsible for those areas. A similar form should be used by each of these managers to measure the performance of their areas against projected objectives. This is critical in the case of the sales force.

After measuring monthly and quarterly objectives against actual results, it is each manager's responsibility to determine why variances have occurred and to take corrective action. If variances remain uncorrected over several periods, the head of the marketing department will need to take forceful action to bring projected and actual results into line. These may involve many alternatives including the replacement of personnel, requesting additional marketing funds from top management, introducing new product lines, lowering prices, and many more.

RESULTS — UNIT SALES — EVALUATION CALENDAR 19___

Review Date	JANUARY		FEBRUARY		MARCH		END 1ST QUARTER	
	Projected Results	Actual Results	Projected Results	Actual Results	Projected Results	Actual Results	Projected Results	Actual Results
All Product Lines — Unit Sales								
Strategically Critical Lines — Unit Sales								
1.								
2.								
3.								
4.								
New Product Lines — Unit Sales								
1.								
2.								
3.								
4.								
Other Product Lines — Unit Sales								
1.								
2.								
3.								
4.								

RESULTS – UNIT SALES – EVALUATION CALENDAR 19___

	Review Date	APRIL		MAY		JUNE		END 2ND QUARTER	
		Projected Results	Actual Results	Projected Results	Actual Results	Projected Results	Actual Results	Projected Results	Actual Results
All Product Lines – Unit Sales									
Strategically Critical Lines – Unit Sales									
1. _____									
2. _____									
3. _____									
4. _____									
New Product Lines – Unit Sales									
1. _____									
2. _____									
3. _____									
4. _____									
Other Product Lines – Unit Sales									
1. _____									
2. _____									
3. _____									
4. _____									

RESULTS – UNIT SALES – EVALUATION CALENDAR 19____

Review Date	JULY		AUGUST		SEPTEMBER		END 3RD QUARTER	
	Projected Results	Actual Results	Projected Results	Actual Results	Projected Results	Actual Results	Projected Results	Actual Results
All Product Lines – Unit Sales								
Strategically Critical Lines – Unit Sales								
1.								
2.								
3.								
4.								
New Product Lines – Unit Sales								
1.								
2.								
3.								
4.								
Other Product Lines – Unit Sales								
1.								
2.								
3.								
4.								

RESULTS – UNIT SALES – EVALUATION CALENDAR 19____

Review Date	OCTOBER		NOVEMBER		DECEMBER		END YEAR	
	Projected Results	Actual Results	Projected Results	Actual Results	Projected Results	Actual Results	Projected Results	Actual Results
All Product Lines – Unit Sales								
Strategically Critical Lines – Unit Sales								
1.								
2.								
3.								
4.								
New Product Lines – Unit Sales								
1.								
2.								
3.								
4.								
Other Product Lines – Unit Sales								
1.								
2.								
3.								
4.								

RESULTS — $ SALES — EVALUATION CALENDAR 19___

	JANUARY		FEBRUARY		MARCH		END 1ST QUARTER	
Review Date	Projected Results	Actual Results	Projected Results	Actual Results	Projected Results	Actual Results	Projected Results	Actual Results
All Product Lines — $ Sales								
Strategically Critical Lines — $ Sales								
1. _____								
2. _____								
3. _____								
4. _____								
New Product Lines — $ Sales								
1. _____								
2. _____								
3. _____								
4. _____								
Other Product Lines — $ Sales								
1. _____								
2. _____								
3. _____								
4. _____								

RESULTS — $ SALES — EVALUATION CALENDAR 19___

	APRIL		MAY		JUNE		END 2ND QUARTER	
Review Date	Projected Results	Actual Results	Projected Results	Actual Results	Projected Results	Actual Results	Projected Results	Actual Results
All Product Lines — $ Sales								
Strategically Critical Lines — $ Sales								
1.								
2.								
3.								
4.								
New Product Lines — $ Sales								
1.								
2.								
3.								
4.								
Other Product Lines — $ Sales								
1.								
2.								
3.								
4.								

RESULTS — $ SALES — EVALUATION CALENDAR 19____

Review Date	JULY		AUGUST		SEPTEMBER		END 3RD QUARTER	
	Projected Results	Actual Results	Projected Results	Actual Results	Projected Results	Actual Results	Projected Results	Actual Results

All Product Lines — $ Sales
Strategically Critical Lines —
$ Sales

1. _____
2. _____
3. _____
4. _____

New Product Lines —
$ Sales

1. _____
2. _____
3. _____
4. _____

Other Product Lines —
$ Sales

1. _____
2. _____
3. _____
4. _____

RESULTS — $ SALES — EVALUATION CALENDAR 19____

Review Date	OCTOBER		NOVEMBER		DECEMBER		END YEAR	
	Projected Results	Actual Results	Projected Results	Actual Results	Projected Results	Actual Results	Projected Results	Actual Results
All Product Lines — $ Sales Strategically Critical Lines — $ Sales								
1. _____								
2. _____								
3. _____								
4. _____								
New Product Lines — $ Sales								
1. _____								
2. _____								
3. _____								
4. _____								
Other Product Lines — $ Sales								
1. _____								
2. _____								
3. _____								
4. _____								

RESULTS — VARIANCE AND CORRECTIONS NEEDED IN EXPECTED AND ACTUAL RESULTS

	Probable Reason for Variance	*Corrective Action to Be Taken*
January		
February		
March		
End 1st Quarter		
April		
May		
June		
End 2nd Quarter		
July		
August		
September		
End 3rd Quarter		
October		
November		
December		
End Year		

END-OF-YEAR REVIEW OF MARKETING PLAN

Problems with development or use of this year's marketing plan.

1. _____

_____

2. _____

_____

3. _____

_____

4. _____

_____

Changes needed to improve the marketing plan for next year.

1. _____

_____

2. _____

_____

3. _____

_____

4. _____

_____

Summary

The use of an operational marketing plan on an annual basis has become a necessity. Today's competitive environment demands a thorough marketing planning process.

An operational marketing plan is designed for use during a fiscal or calendar year. This plan is most effective when it supports a longer-range strategic plan. Generally, strategic planning is conducted by top management with input assistance by staff and middle-level management.

A carefully constructed operational marketing plan can assist upper management as a tool during the process of strategic planning. However, the primary purpose of an operational marketing plan is to plan and direct field marketing operations.

The marketing planning process does not end with an operational marketing plan. Each functional area such as advertising, sales promotion, and sales should develop and use a one-year plan. Finally, the success of each salesperson depends on planning one's territory. Market success does not simply *happen* at any level; *it is planned.*

Realistic objectives can be established only after careful analysis. Alternative options for accomplishing these objectives must then be evaluated. Operational strategies result from this selection process. An operational marketing plan will clearly describe the resources needed to accomplish strategies, and the time frame in which they will be required.

Marketing planning never ends. Operational marketing plans view twelve future months. A new plan must be developed months before the current one expires.

Marketing plans that are written and then relegated to a shelf represent wasted effort. The process of developing "Winning Marketing Plans" continuously evolves. The basic format described in this workbook will change very little, but techniques for developing a plan change through technology and the level of expertise and experience of those writing the plans.

The widespread use of personal computers currently presents an opportunity for marketing planners to customize and store the marketing plan format for instant retrieval and modification.

Marketing planning remains a new and often fearful experience for many. The "marketing concept" has not been accepted by all organizations. Marketing planning, sales, advertising, and other related functions remain organizationally separated in too many enterprises. Despite a desperate need for a market consumer-driven philosophy, some companies continue to view marketing as solely the sales arm to "peddle" products or services designed and produced to meet the organization's capabilities and desires.

Marketing planning offers opportunities within all organizations to foster teamwork and to develop an awareness of the need for cooperation and planning among different functional areas.

The process of developing a marketing plan is never easy. Many consider it to be the least desirable of all marketing responsibilities. This workbook was designed to assist with the task and to insure that critical areas are not overlooked.

The future of a fast-moving, competitive society depends upon planning. Effective marketing, enhanced by a professional marketing plan, will help to create a sound future for all who are affected by the strength or weakness, failure or success of an enterprise.